WHAT TRUSTED PROF
ARE SHARING AFTER READING
BRINGING IN THE BUSINESS

"Shift your sales mindset and see incredible results with *Bringing In The Business*! Focusing on creating lasting relationships through enrollment, *Bringing In The Business* is a powerful guide to long-term growth and your success."

Dr. Marshall Goldsmith,
Thinkers50 #1 Executive Coach and *New York Times* best-selling author of *The Earned Life, Triggers,* and *What Got You Here Won't Get You There*

"*Bringing In The Business* hits the crux of what business is all about. Often the process causes fear or insecurity in new salespeople and even seasoned sales leaders. These authors have written the four phases that occur over dynamic and thoughtful conversations that will lead to your success."

Ann Dugan, Founder,
Institute for Entrepreneurial Excellence (IEE),
University of Pittsburgh

"*Bringing In The Business* is insightful and contains practical advice that helps demystify the complicated world of business development. It will help you focus on providing solutions instead of merely trying to make a sale."

Sean Smith,
Chief Marketing Officer,
Schneider Downs

"*Bringing In The Business* takes selling and makes it a process that requires no selling. It's all about conversations, asking questions, listening carefully and paying attention to details. I have been in sales most of my adult life and read many sales books. None take you through the process that creates a real relationship, based on trust and mutual respect, like this book does."

Dick Singer, Master Chair,
Vistage Worldwide; President, RDS Associates LLC

"In my own work I say, 'the key to connection is conversation. The secret of conversation is asking questions.' David, Henry, and Mark explain the different types of questions to ask, and in what order to ask them, to win the clients we strive for. *Bringing In The Business* is a book to yellow highlight and add Post-its. Keep close to hand before every call."

Patricia Fripp, Past President,
National Speakers Association,
author of *Deliver Unforgettable Presentations*

"As an entrepreneur, I've been in 'sales' and marketing my entire life. This book will explain the process of how you can be more clear in your communications and focused on what matters in your conversations. Buy it. Read it. Use it."

Thomas Freyvogel, entrepreneur,
business developer, and consultant

"First, I love this book. It took me back to when we met with you. I literally visualized being in that seat again and how it felt to engage, or should I say be 'enrolled.' It was a conversation, safe, and the questions you asked helped us be clearer about what we really needed and wanted. I love that this book is a guide, you can pick it up over and over and focus on the part of the process you are currently in and apply the tips in real time. This book will serve as my bible of sorts for establishing high-paying clients and having successful conversations that lead to meaningful client engagements."

Jessica Brooks, consultant and former
President and CEO of the Pittsburgh
Business Group on Health

"David Goldman has done it again. With his second book, *Bringing In The Business Without Sounding Like A Salesperson*, he and coauthors Henry DeVries and Mark LeBlanc have given you an outline for business development success. Place this one on your short list."

Steve Irwin, Partner,
Leech Tishman Fuscaldo & Lampl LLC

Position Yourself
As A Trusted Professional

BRINGING IN THE BUSINESS

Without Sounding Like A Salesperson

DAVID GOLDMAN, HENRY DEVRIES, AND MARK LEBLANC

INDIE BOOKS
INTERNATIONAL

Defining Statement™, Defining Paragraph™, and Defining Story™ are pending trademarks of Mark A. LeBlanc.

ISBN- 13: 978-1-95765-14-15
Library of Congress Control Number: 2023908302

Cover design by Laura Duffy Design
Interior design by Amit Dey

INDIE BOOKS INTERNATIONAL®, INC.
2511 WOODLANDS WAY
OCEANSIDE, CA 92054
www.indiebooksintl.com

CONTENTS

PREFACE

By Mark A. LeBlanc, CSP, CPAE

I have been on my own virtually my entire life. I had a job once for about six months, and I was inspired by the words, "You're fired!" I was twenty-one years old, and my future seemed questionable at best.

As luck or fate would have it, I received an invitation in the mail that was a direct mail piece announcing a two-day sales seminar. The trainer was Don Sheehan and he had written a book titled, *Shut Up and Sell!*

That experience would put me on a path of continuous learning from some of the industry's best and brightest when it comes to marketing, sales, and business development. I made a vow to do whatever it would take to make it on my own. I am celebrating my fortieth year of being my own boss.

I met my coauthors David Goldman in 1996, and Henry DeVries in 2000. All three of us have been lifelong learners when it comes to the art, skill, and science of selling. I think I write for all of us when I say we have listened, learned, applied, failed, and succeeded along the way. Our learning came one conversation at a time over years and decades.

It only made sense that we would come together to write a book on how not to sound like a salesperson. Believe it or not, we hear that excuse day in and day out from emerging and seasoned veterans of business, especially when it comes to people in professional services.

Why is it that some people sell without ever sounding and acting like a salesperson, while others make the act a dreadful process? It can be an incredible experience when you are in the presence of a true professional, or as Jeff Thull, author of *Mastering the Complex Sale*, would suggest, a prime resource instead of a pest or peddler.

Selling is nothing more than a communication process, and it begins and ends with a conversation. In some instances, it may be a series of conversations or one conversation that contains several sub-conversations.

When you understand the different types of conversations and how to navigate them with confidence, you will find yourself creating more agreements. Some might say you will close more sales. We believe in creating agreements that honor an individual, establish trust, and build respect throughout the entire process. When you do it well, you will put yourself in a position to receive more referrals, which is the dream of every business professional.

Think of the last time you bought a new car or needed legal representation. You might love your new car, and yet, the experience of buying the car was negative. When that happens, how likely are you to refer a friend, family member, or colleague to that dealership? Or, you may have won the case in court, and yet, you would not dream of making a referral to your attorney. There is a reason.

In your hands you hold the ideas and insights for making the process enjoyable. It doesn't include making a deal, reducing your fee, or throwing in the kitchen sink. It does require you to read with an open mind, a notebook and something to write with. Keep this book handy and refer to it often. You will develop a philosophy and an approach to doing business that will set you apart from your competition and position yourself as outstanding in your chosen field.

As you explore the different types of conversations and traverse the four phases of the marketing and selling process, never forget that the best conversations include more questions, and if you listen more than fifty-one percent of the time, your odds of a favorable result go way up.

Listening is the greatest gift you can give another person at home and in the marketplace. You will never forget the professional from any walk of business who asked the right questions, listened carefully, and responded appropriately. The odds are good, when given the opportunity – you helped get the word out about him or her.

Mark LeBlanc, CSP, CPAE
Author of *Never Be the Same*
and *Growing Your Business!*

1

WHY ENROLLMENT IS IMPORTANT

Do you sell, or do you enroll?

If you want to attract more high-paying clients, a great deal is riding on your answer.

Prospective clients do not want to be sold; they want to buy. If you can learn how to enroll people, you will be able to get more clients without having them feel like you are selling them at all.

The word *enrollment* is often associated with a college or private school process for admitting students. Sometimes it is tied to recruiting volunteers for a worthwhile endeavor. That is the mindset you want to project. Like a college dean (Henry was one), you want to have enrollment conversations.

Some critics will say differentiating the words *selling* and *enrolling* is just semantics, merely wordplay for the same strategy and tactics. It's not; there's a difference.

In fact, it really *is* about mindset. One reason the "selling" mindset is distasteful to you is that it puts the burden on you.

You need to convince someone about your service or ability to solve a problem.

The distinction of "enrollment" puts the onus on the prospective client. They have an issue that they want to have handled and they are looking for the best solution.

Or perhaps they want to find a service professional to be on their team.

The mindset shift is that instead of selling, you offer them an opportunity to buy. Let us repeat – People don't want to be sold; they want to buy what they want.

For many consultants, professionals, and entrepreneurs, how to attract clients can't be explained, which is understandable. We have interviewed hundreds of people who gave us some variation of what we call The Great Work Myth. It is a flawed ideal. It is the notion that, *If you do great work, clients will find you.*

Offering a great service is not good enough. You need to learn the subtle art of enrolling clients through conversations.

Let us three authors give credit where credit is due. Our thinking has been influenced by the teachings of author David Maister, retired Harvard Business School professor;[1] Tony Alessandra, author of *Non-Manipulative Selling*[2] and *The Platinum Rule*;[3] Bill Baron, Patrick Dominguez, and Kevin Cullen, thought leaders in mastering enrollment; Jeff Thull, author of *Mastering the Complex Sale*;[4] Tom Searcy, author of *Whale Hunting*;[5] and author David Sandler, founder of Sandler Sales Training.[6]

You have an opportunity to get better at enrolling people through engaging conversations. The prize is great because enrollment can multiply the number of conversations you have with potential high-paying people and increase your conversion rates. The time is now to learn the subtle art of enrollment conversations.

2

HOW SMART PROFESSIONALS ENROLL

Offering a great product or service is not enough.

Success in business extends beyond offering a top-notch product or service. Many professionals are averse to being perceived as salespeople, preferring to grow their businesses, expand their clientele, and receive referrals without the stigma of "selling."

The good news is that acquiring high-paying clients is less about sales and more about a process of enrollment. The question then becomes, how can you effectively guide potential clients through this journey?

At your best, you enroll individuals into the *possibility* that your product or service can transform their lives. This process unfolds through four distinct phases: the attraction phase, the meaningful conversation phase, the decision phase, and the agreement phase. As you progress through these phases, your chances of success and the potential for lasting relationships multiply in your favor.

Attraction Phase: Begin by introducing yourself and your work in a way that captures interest. When asked, 'What do you do?' respond with a phrase that magnetizes your ideal clients towards you, piquing their curiosity.

Meaningful Conversation Phase: This is usually the first, official meeting with a potential client. During these interactions, establish a foundation of rapport. It need not be complex or time-consuming. Initiating with a question like, "Why did you want to meet with me today?" lays the groundwork for your relationship. Within this phase, three vital sub-conversations emerge:

1. **The Conversation For Possibility:** This is the pivotal step, creating the possibility that your product or service could meet their needs. This conversation must come from the other person, not you. Ask questions that uncover desired outcomes, deepen the connection, and strengthen the relationship.

2. **The Conversation For Value:** Here, the other person reveals the value of achieving their goals. Inquire, "What would it be worth to you in real terms, in your life, if I can help you make your dreams a reality?" Get a real number. This insight is important in the discussion about fees.

3. **The Conversation For Opportunity:** Now, you get to talk about your program or service, aligning it with the person's needs and desires. You also are assessing if your offering aligns with their goals. If it's not a fit, gracefully suggest an alternative resource.

Decision Phase: This is where you issue the call to action. Regardless of how smoothly the previous phases went, you must ask for the business. Be prepared to answer questions and gauge their readiness with a question like, "Does this make sense?" or "Are you ready to start?"

Agreement Phase: Once the person signals readiness, you enter the Agreement Phase. Here, discuss scope, options, fees, and terms. The enrollment process is not complete until both parties agree, either verbally or in writing, to commence working together. Often, this results in an invoice for the fee or a deposit to initiate the process. Managing this phase effectively fosters trust and frequently leads to more referrals.

The secret to generating referrals lies in your client's satisfaction with the enrollment process and their delight in your services. Meeting the best of what your client needs and wants, becomes the cornerstone of your relationship. It's the difference between having a satisfied client who never refers you and having an enthusiastic client who becomes a champion for your services.

In summary, success in attracting high-paying clients lies in the art of enrollment, not traditional sales. It's about inviting, not selling.

Listen Carefully And Respond Appropriately
By Mark LeBlanc, CSP, CPAE

When you list all of the skills necessary to succeed in your career, the skill I would rank number one is listening. Do you remember taking a listening course or class in high school or college or any secondary learning institution? Usually not. I was fortunate to meet, listen to, and learn from Dr. Lyman K. (Manny) Steil when I was twenty-two years old. I have been blessed to call him a friend and mentor for over forty years.

Manny is considered one of the foremost experts on listening around the world. He has spoken, consulted, and written on communication and specifically listening for over fifty years. He impressed upon me the importance of listening at an early stage of my development, and it is a skill I continue to sharpen even today. When I listen well and respond appropriately, it is as if I am charting a course to respect, trust, and honor with the people I serve. If I listen, respond, or react poorly, I am at risk of losing the sale and opportunity for my next lifelong relationship.

Over time, as I began to improve my skill, I noticed four mindsets in the people I interacted with and served. I heard a thinking mindset, a doing mindset, a struggling mindset, and an achieving mindset. Unlike a personality profile assessment, it became clear to me that we all move among these four mindsets on a daily basis depending on what the task or challenge is before us in the moment. It even worked at home with my wife or with my parents, nieces, and nephews.

In the next seventy-two hours, no matter who you are engaged in a conversation with, listen carefully and he or she will reveal their current mindset in less than sixty seconds. Armed with a simple response, you will increase the likelihood of a positive result, or you may put a ding into your relationship.

When you hear, *I am thinking about…*or *I was wondering…*or *I am considering…*you get the idea. You are engaged with another person who is a Thinker. Slow down and make sure you are answering their questions, satisfying their concerns, and providing them with the information they need to make a better decision.

When you hear, *I want to get started…*or *we would like to be up and running by the end of the year…*or *how soon can we get started* – you are in a conversation with a Doer. Focus your responses with one or two action items, a sense of urgency, and a spirit of enthusiasm.

When you hear at the beginning of your conversation, *how much will this cost…*or *how long with this take…* or anything that resembles doubt or uncertainty, you are possibly with a Struggler. A Struggler is not a bad person, nor is it a consistent mindset. The other person may be having a hard time, not able to see the bigger picture, or may have been upset, hurt, or burned by another service provider. In that moment, you have the ability to convey optimism, a can-do attitude and "I've got your back" mentality – you are taking their moment of challenge and turning it into an ocean of possibility.

When you hear, *we are looking for someone to work with…*or *we need to work together…we want someone we can add to our team* – you are in conversation with an Achiever. An Achiever likes to think things through before they decide, and once they make a decision, they are focused on doing the right things in the right order. When a problem or obstacle arises, they shift into a creative or brainstorming moment to explore how to move through a valley or challenge. Achievers put together a plan to keep them focused and on track, surrounding themselves with the right resources, advisors, and partners for the long term.

Before you write this information off as too simplistic, give it a whirl. In time, I expect you will create magic in your work and home life. It might be my most important concept or the one thing that has helped me be not only successful, but significant with the people I interact with often or even on rare occasions.

Bonus Phase: Referrals

Getting referrals is easier when the enrollment process is smooth, and you help the client produce the results they are seeking.

Remember that you control the enrollment process, but the other person controls the answers. When done correctly, the other person feels in control during the entire enrollment process. A positive emotional feeling can result in generating referrals.

You want them to feel you really understand them, and that they are seen and heard. They also must feel you have a proven process for solving problems like theirs. Then they are usually much more open to and happy to refer you.

Enroll On!
By David Goldman

It was June 1989, in a Chicago, Illinois, hotel ballroom, theater seating. I was one of 120 participants in a leadership development program where we were learning how to be leaders in front of a room. And this was the enrollment weekend. We were going to learn how to enroll someone into the possibility of what their life could be. Sounds very exciting.

I came into the sales arena in the 1970s in what is known as the J. Douglas Edwards era, which I define as, "You have my money in your pocket, and my job is to get it." It was very confrontational, almost combative. It was certainly argumentative. I hated it. I got pretty good at it, mind you, but I never liked it.

The technique was that in an hour-long presentation, there was no questioning. There was no interviewing the person; you were putting on a show. So, in the first twenty minutes you would scare the heck out of the person and let them know why they needed your product.

The Sandler Selling System talks about pain. This tactic uses out and out fear. After scaring the prospect for about twenty minutes, you'd spend maybe ten or fifteen minutes describing why your product was the absolute solution for them. And then you'd have to leave at least half an hour for what was affectionately called the close. And in that J. Douglas Edwards model, you had to deal with objections. A sales pro would have six answers to every objection you would hear.

The good news is there were only about five objections you could hear. People either weren't interested, they had to think about it, they had to talk to somebody about it, or they couldn't afford it, which by the way is a real objection. Or they thought they were already okay, and they were satisfied with the status quo.

In fact, if you could get the other person to move from one objection to another, you had them on the run and now you "had 'em." Ugh!

Back to Chicago.

We got to the point in the seminar where we were discussing how to deal with objections. "Here we go," I thought. All that former training came flooding back into my head. However, one of the agreements of the course was to look at life with an open mind—true possibility thinking. As if that concept could shift the way you live your life.

Our weekend leader, Kevin Cullen, was a master at enrollment. He asked for a volunteer to come up to the platform and demonstrate (role-play) their least favorite objection.

He was going to show us how to handle it.

A woman from Colorado volunteered and her least favorite objection was, "I'm not interested." Kevin brought this woman up to the platform and said, "I'm going to be you. And you're going to be the toughest prospect you've ever had. And tell me you're not interested." She agreed.

Kevin invited her to enroll in the program. And she said in a big, tough voice, "I'm not interested." And Kevin looked her right in the eye and sincerely said, "Oh, well, tell me, what are you interested in?"

You know, there are moments when your life changes in an instant. And you know, in that instant, that your life has changed. I like to call them magic moments. And at that moment, my life changed. I transformed my sales. I transformed my results. I transformed my life.

Imagine you could actually have a conversation with somebody and find out what they're interested in—how simple, how incredible; you didn't have to be combative at all.

Later on, I found out that you could actually have that conversation upfront, not wait for the close. You could engage with a person, engage with the client upfront to find out what they wanted. And that, in fact, was the birth of the enrollment process.

I have three questions for you:

1. What beliefs, habits, and patterns of thinking are you stuck in that might be holding you back?
2. Are you open to looking at things differently?
3. What are you interested in?

3

THE ATTRACTION PHASE

'Tis a gift to be simple, 'tis a gift to be clear (with apologies to the Shaker folk song).

The goal of the attraction phase is to get a potential client's ear, attention, or eye on your business.

You must be clear during the attraction phase. If you want to attract high-paying clients, you need to clearly describe what you do and how you can best benefit a potential client.

Based on our hundreds of interviews with top professionals, these conversations are especially critical for those who serve in roles such as chief executive officer, general manager, principal, partner, or head of an office, business unit, or practice for professional service firms, especially in the fields of accounting, dental consulting, financial services, management consulting, marketing and advertising, executive search services, software development, technology services, and law.

These professionals think of these attraction phase conversations, as one professional put it, "as starting to dance with a potential client to see if romance develops."

Enroll On!

By Henry DeVries

Here are the top ways to generate attraction conversations.

According to former Harvard Business School professor David Maister, typical marketing practices are not only inapplicable to professional service firms, but they may be dangerously wrong.

Many professionals are frustrated with the quality of their business development materials, they are concerned with their firm's low profile, or they feel pressure because their efforts are not generating enough new client leads. Are you experiencing any of these issues?

Many professionals do not know there is a body of knowledge about what does and does not work in marketing professional services. My own thirty years of practical experience in marketing professional service firms supports these findings. The best marketing for professional service firms is educational in nature. Here are the top fourteen tactics that work, in order from the least to the most effective:

The Inadequate Seven

14. Cold calling—This should be done by a business-development person, never a principal. A better approach is what I call warm calling, which is following up with workshop and seminar invitations.

13. Video brochures—These can be great lead conversion tools, but they cost too much for lead generation. Instead, stick the videos on your website.

12. Printed brochures—Again, don't spend too much money upfront to generate leads. Instead, create these as PDF files that can be read using Adobe Acrobat and place them on your website.

11. Sponsorship of cultural/sports events—Being the title sponsor of the right event can have an impact, but it is not the best use of your lead generation dollars.

10. Advertising—Isn't it ironic that none of the great advertising agencies built their clientele by advertising? However, if you specialize in an industry and it publishes directories, it is always good to have your firm included.

9. Direct mail—This is the traditional direct mail of a letter and a printed piece like a response card. Some accountants and financial planners have used this cost-effectively, maybe offering a complimentary consultation. (There is a much better form of direct mail; see tactic No. 1.)

8. Publicity—While getting your name in the newspaper and trade journals is a cost-effective way to increase awareness about your firm, it doesn't always translate into business.

The Magnificent Seven

7. Paid ballroom workshops—Rent out the ballroom at the local Marriott or Hilton and charge for an all-day or half-day seminar. Participants should take away a substantial packet of good information from your firm (and enjoy a good meal too).

6. Tips e-newsletters—This is the water drip torture school of marketing and the opposite of spam. By signing up for your newsletter lists, people are telling you they are interested in what you have to say but are not yet ready for a relationship. These people should receive valuable, how-to information and event invitations from you on a monthly basis until they decide to opt out of the list.

5. Networking and trade shows—An excellent way to gather business cards and ask for permission to include people on your e-newsletter list.

4. Community and association involvement—Everyone likes to do business with people they know, like, and trust. You need to get involved and circulate to percolate.

3. How-to articles in target-rich, client-oriented press—Better than any brochure is the how-to article that appears in a publication your target audience reads.

2. How-to showcase speeches at target-rich, client industry meetings—People want to hire experts,

and an expert by definition is someone who is invited to speak. Actively seek out forums to speak and list past and future speaking dates on your website.

1. Free or low-cost small-scale seminars—The best proactive tactic you can employ is to regularly invite people by mail and email to small seminars or group consultations. If your potential clients are spread out geographically, you can do these briefings via the internet (webinars) or on Zoom (we call them Zoominars). These can't be ninety-minute commercials. You need to present valuable information about how to solve the problems your potential clients are facing, and then include a little mention of your services.

Nearly everything you do from a marketing perspective serves the attraction phase. Developing a messaging platform, creating marketing tools, and executing marketing strategies are built with one purpose in mind: to attract more potential clients.

Your potential clients come into your world in various ways. Depending on your business model, they may walk into your place of business, call you, or send you an email. They may find you via Facebook, Twitter, or LinkedIn. Or you might engage them by means of the fourteen tactics listed above.

No matter how you attract potential clients, you must be prepared with something good to say.

Create A Defining Statement

This is a simple answer to a simple question, "What do you do?"

Most people answer the question by title; most titles turn off the audience. "I'm a lawyer." "I'm a financial advisor." "I'm a coach." "I'm a consultant."

Think of it like bait on the hook when you are fly fishing. This is something you toss out there to see if it gets a nibble. Very few titles create a bite.

Better to answer by concept. The easiest way to position yourself by concept is to create what Mark calls a great defining statement.

When you can answer the question in a simple, succinct, and concise way, you will attract more potential clients.

One approach to creating a Defining Statement involves the "Magic Triangle of Marketing."

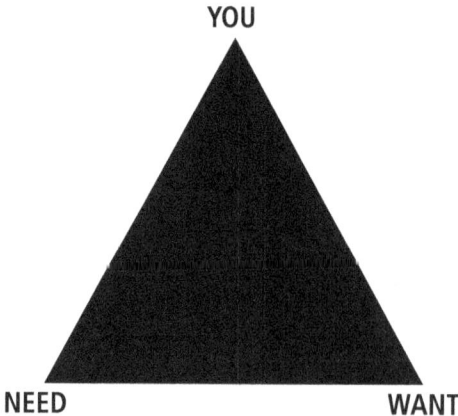

At the top of the triangle is **YOU –** the person sitting in your chair. There are two categories for YOU. First, you are doing what you love to do. We assume that is true. If it is not true, then that is a whole different program called, "Finding what you love to do." Second, you are working with people you like to work with. That is where you need to do some home-work. You must determine who is a "perfect fit." We encour-age clients to write down twenty characteristics of what a perfect fit would be for you. Some ideas include gender, age range, geography, income level, personality type, outlook on life, attitude, demeanor, occupation, health status, etc. These aren't the same for everyone. One area to investigate is who are your favorite clients and what do they have in common? Who your right-fit (ten characteristics) or perfect-fit (twenty characteristics) clients are will help you craft your defining statement. (see Appendix A)

One of the lower points of the triangle is **NEED**. Again, we assume you believe that people need your product or service. However, people don't buy what they need; they buy what they **WANT.** That is the third point of the triangle and another key element of your defining statement. Once you determine who is your perfect fit—your ideal client—you must figure out what they want! Then your Defining Statement (the answer to the question, "What do you do?") will read, "I work with _____ who want _____."

For example, Mark's is, "I work with business owners who want to grow their business." David's is, "I work with professional service providers who want to bring in more business." Henry's is, "I work with agency owners and strategic consultants who want to attract high-paying clients by market-ing with a book and a speech."

It is not easy. In fact, it may be one of the hardest exercises you will undertake in your business. The rewards can be great. Here are examples to help you understand what makes a good defining statement.

Consultant Examples

I work with business owners who want to accelerate their results and grow their business.

I work with leaders who want to develop stronger teams and get their people behind a common goal.

Financial Advisor Examples

I work with people who want to accumulate wealth and make sure it's distributed the way they want.

I work with young people who want to start investing in the market and build a foundation for wealth.

Real Estate Agent Examples

I work with people who want to buy their first home and sellers who want top dollar for their property.

I work with homeowners on how to maximize their property value and look for investment opportunities.

Bottom line: focus on the dream of your potential clients and the people you serve best. Some prefer, and will tell you, to take a pain or problem-focused approach to your statement. It can work, as we like to live in a world of two or more right answers. We feel that creating a dream-focused Defining Statement is more likely to get the ear of your prospective client.

Dennis
by David Goldman

In 1995, I met Dennis at a networking event. As a financial advisor with a major insurance company, he was doing well but not great. He knew he could be doing better and didn't know how or what was missing. He hired me to coach him with a goal of doubling his income. Dennis had a great work ethic which means he was willing to put in long hours to get the result. However, he was disorganized and had no format for his meetings. His strategy was to spray and pray and put in ten-, twelve-, and sometimes sixteen-hour days.

We worked extensively on the attraction phase and meaningful conversation phase of his business. We created a great Defining Statement for him, and he started to use it.

It wasn't easy at first. The shift in mindset from talking about himself, the company, and what he could do for someone, to finding out what the potential client wanted and how he could help them get it, was tough. In addition, the concept of "the narrower your focus; the broader your appeal" was hard for Dennis to adopt.

Finally, he started to break through and practice his new defining statement consistently and employ the enrollment process every time. In six months, his income increased from $4,000 per month to $6,500 per month. Dennis hired me for another six-month agreement, and we continued to refine his approach and first meeting strategy. He also tightened his decision and agreement phase conversation.

At the end of the second six months, Dennis's income was $10,500 per month.

Over the following fifteen years, Dennis's income increased ten-fold and he now enjoys a lifestyle that he always wanted and a thriving business that supports it.

Two More Attraction Phase Tools:

This is not your grandfather's elevator pitch.

In addition to the defining statement, it pays to have a defining paragraph and a defining story. These are a little more elaborate than the defining statement when you have more time to talk about who you are and what you do.

Remember, the goal of the attraction phase is to get a potential client's ear, attention, or eye on your business.

Craft Your Defining Paragraph

Include your defining paragraph in all your attraction phase materials and networking. Follow this seven-sentence framework to craft your defining paragraph:

1. Your name
2. Your company's name
3. Defining statement for your primary area of expertise
4. Defining statement for your secondary area of expertise
5. Credibility statement
6. Value statement
7. Approachability statement

Commit this structure to memory. You need to see it in your mind's eye. You will come to rely on it in a multitude of situations.

Here is an example from a financial advisor:

1. My name is Bob Johnson.
2. I run a company called Smart Money Solutions.
3. I work with couples that want to get on the same page regarding their finances and improve their net worth.
4. In addition, I conduct presentations on how to distribute wealth to your loved ones or charity.
5. In fact, I am a frequent guest on podcasts and media interviews.
6. As a result of my work, clients often share that they reduce their debt, protect their assets, and experience real peace of mind regarding their retirement.
7. On a personal note, my wife and I enjoy traveling in our RV and eating at restaurants featured on *Diners, Drive-ins and Dives*.

Craft Your Defining Story

The next tool you need is your defining story. Remember, human brains are hardwired for stories. This is a two-minute tale that explains why you do what you do. It leaves bread crumbs on how you can help them.

The Simple Six-Step Heroic Storytelling Formula
By Henry DeVries

Storytelling helps persuade people on an emotional level. Discoveries in neuroscience prove decisions are made on the basis of emotion, not logic. So how do you persuade the emotional part of the person's brain?

Humans are hardwired for stories. If you want the person to think it over, give them lots of facts and figures. If you want them to decide to hire you, tell them the right story.

My research at the New Client Marketing Institute revealed the two biggest factors for gaining credibility with someone are the quality of questions you ask during the meaningful conversation and your ability to tell a true under-two-minute story of how you have taken someone like them from a problem to success.

Think of these stories like a two-minute movie you are creating in the mind of the person. You want them to project themselves into the story.

Today, any professional can tell a great story by using proven techniques employed by Hollywood, Madison Avenue, and Wall Street by using "The Simple Six-Step Heroic Storytelling Formula."

These stories must be true case studies but told in a certain way. Here is a quick overview of the formula:

1. **Start with a main character**. Every story starts with the name of a character who wants something. This

is your client. Make your main characters likeable so the listeners will root for them. To make them likeable, describe some of their good qualities or attributes. Generally, three attributes work best: "Marie was smart, tough, and fair" or "Johan was hardworking, caring, and passionate." For privacy reasons, do not use their real names. ("This is a true story, but the names have been changed to protect confidentiality.")

2. **Have a nemesis character**. Stories need conflict to be interesting. What person, institution, or condition stands in the character's way? The villain in the story might be a challenge in the business environment, such as the recession of 2008 or the Affordable Care Act. (The government is always a classic nemesis character.)

3. **Bring in a mentor character**. Heroes need help on their journey. They need to work with a wise person. This is where you come in. Be the voice of wisdom and experience. The hero does not succeed alone; they succeed because of the help you provide.

4. **Know what story you are telling**. Human brains are programmed to relate to one of eight great metastories. These are: monster, underdog, comedy, tragedy, mystery, quest, rebirth, and escape. If the story is about overcoming a huge problem, that is a monster problem story. If the company was like a David that overcame an industry Goliath, that is an underdog story.

5. **Have the hero succeed**. Typically, the main character needs to succeed, with one exception: tragedy. The tragic story is told as a cautionary tale. Great for teaching lessons but not great for attracting clients. Have the hero go from mess to success, i.e., it was a struggle, and they couldn't have done it without you.

6. **Give the listeners the moral of the story.** Take a cue from Aesop, the man who gave us fables like "The Tortoise and the Hare." (The moral: slow and steady wins the race.) Don't count on the listeners to get the message. The storyteller's final job is to tell them what the story means.

Here are four perfect attraction phase opportunities to persuade with your defining story:

To Intrigue A Client During A Meeting

Never lead with your defining story. First have a conversation with your potential client. Don't randomly tell stories, but instead use stories at strategic moments. Ask about their goals, what they are doing right, and what they see as the roadblocks they hope you can help them get past. At this point ask, "May I tell you a true story about how we helped a client get from where you are now to where you want to go?"

On Your Website Or LinkedIn Profile

Get rid of that boring bio. Use a compelling defining story.

In Collateral Material

Don't just tell, when stories will sell. In your brochures and information kits, replace drab case histories with persuasive defining stories.

During A Speech, Media Interview, Or Job Interview

Occasionally, you might get an invitation to make a speech, give an interview to the media, or interview for a job. Illustrate your message with your pithy story.

Bottom line: Told at the right time, a defining story can advance the conversation from the attraction phase to the meaningful conversation phase. Or it can move you from the meaningful conversation to a positive decision.

For more detail, we refer you to the book *Defining You*.[7]

Have People Experience You

People experience you in a presentation, whether it's hearing a speech you give, networking at an event, or meeting you at a trade show. You might have a YouTube channel, an audio or video podcast, or a blog. Always favor marketing strategies in the attraction phase where people experience you, because that's where the magic happens. Be prepared with something good to say.

Mark's Virtual Coffee Strategy

While there are a number of ways you could navigate this strategy, whether in person or virtual, Mark will make sure it is never a selling zone. If every lasting relationship starts with a conversation, then he feels there is no need to make a sale at this point, even if a prospective client wants to buy.

It is certainly contrary to every old, tired, and traditional form of selling or the ABC (Always Be Closing) approach to making sales.

According to Mark, if you show up, be present, listen carefully, and be as helpful as you can be – that's when the magic happens and the road to trust is established.

"My benchmark is two coffee-talks per week or eight every thirty days. More than 90 percent of these conversations are across the lens using Zoom."

His approach is simple. He will thank the person for taking the time to meet. His only agenda is to hear a person's story, listen carefully, and answer any questions they might have. If a person is interested in knowing more about his work or hiring him, Mark will schedule a second conversation. In between, he may mail a book or provide additional resources or tools of value. It clearly draws a line or boundary between a get-to-know you conversation and a bona fide selling or enrollment conversation.

The exception to this approach is when a person Mark knows has a high degree of knowledge of his work or maybe has heard Mark speak, or specifically asks for a conversation to explore working with him, he may choose to combine the two conversations.

For coauthor Henry, who works with agency owners and strategic consultants who want to attract high-paying clients by marketing with a book and a speech, he offers no-cost strategy calls that he named BookChats. His BookChats are no-selling-zone attraction phase conversations.

Henry's agenda for the call is to help the potential author gain clarity around four topics:

- What is their goal for writing a book?
- What assets do they have, like blogs and articles, for writing a book?
- What roadblocks do they see hindering them in writing and publishing a book?
- Would they like to know how others have gotten from where they are to where they want to go?

Henry does not have a meaningful conversation about how he helps people unless the person specifically asks.

You want to hear their story. You want to listen carefully. You want to answer any questions they might have. You just want to be as helpful as you can be.

Now let's take you behind the curtain. Even when we say we have no real agenda, isn't there always an agenda? Your agenda is to establish rapport so they will ask for the next step, the next conversation, which is the meaningful conversation. That conversation is the focus of the next chapter.

4

THE MEANINGFUL CONVERSATION PHASE

The meaningful conversation phase is where you've gotten permission to meet following the attraction phase, where a potential client has raised his or her hand.

That's worth repeating: never start the enrollment process until you are asked or given permission. Often, this is the initial meeting with the potential client.

During the attraction phase, you told them who you are, what you do, and for whom you do it. Then, you found that they were interested in talking further. Now, you are actually qualifying a person in order to determine if the person could be a good-fit, right-fit, or perfect-fit client and relationship.

Once a prospective client is comfortable with you and is confident you might be the right resource or trusted professional, then you have an opportunity to build your case leading to a yes or no client engagement.

Many lawyers, financial advisors, and other professional service providers are trained to tell prospective clients who they are, what they do, how they do it, and how they get paid. That is the basic first interview. Occasionally, the advisor will mention the features and benefits of what they do and think it's a whole new level of sophistication, above and beyond the norm. The entire conversation is focused on the service provider and is self-serving.

The enrollment process shifts the focus from the professional provider to the prospective client and what he or she wants. The difference is remarkable.

Dick

By David Goldman

The year was 2009, one year after the largest financial crisis since the Great Depression that lasted through the 1930s. Dick, a financial advisor with a legal background, operated in a highly specialized marketplace that highlighted his expertise. Dick was doing well and knew he could be doing much better. He just didn't know how, so he hired me.

Like most attorneys, Dick was trained to talk about himself, his expertise, his accomplishments, his technical ability, his process, and how he got paid. What was missing was the client and what the client wanted.

There must be a shift in mindset from you to the client. Please allow us to explain why this shift is difficult at first. In addition to the years of training and experience of doing things in a particular way, it's hard to listen to someone as if it's the first time you have heard it. After one has been in business for a while, there is very little you haven't heard.

When someone starts to tell you their issue or what they want, it's easy to rush to a solution and talk about your process. Even worse, it's easy to assume what they want without even asking. After all, you *have* heard it before. However, unless you listen to the prospective client and their issue or desire, you risk missing the mark. You could be wrong – not likely, but it could happen. More importantly, listening and really understanding the client creates a bond that is difficult to break. It's the first step to creating a client for life.

The Goldman Enrollment Process provides a format that forces the professional to consider the client first and allows for the shift in mindset. When Dick employed it, his results skyrocketed. Within a year, Dick's revenue increased from low- to mid-six figures to a consistent seven figure income. He hasn't looked back since.

There are five steps to the Goldman Enrollment Process:

Step 1: The Background Of Relationship

First and foremost, there must be some background of relationship. Some rapport must be established. This doesn't have to be elaborate, nor does it have to take a great deal of time. Without it, however, nothing will go further. It could be from an introduction or from a referral from someone else. It could be from meeting someone at a function or a business gathering. It could even be from a completely unknown source. But there must be a relationship.

You can establish this with a simple question. Ask, "Why did you want to meet today?" Then listen. That will be enough to establish there is a relationship.

Step 2: The Conversation For Possibility

This is the most important part of the process. The entire enrollment hinges on this piece. That might seem like a contradiction since we said nothing happens without the background of relationship. While that's true, once there is a relationship, *possibility* is the most important part of the process.

The conversation for possibility is simply establishing the possibility that your product or service could be for someone. This is where the entire reason for your service is brought to light, in complete detail. In fact, the more said about the possibility of your offering, the better. Here's the catch: the conversation for possibility must come from the potential client's mouth. You must ask the kinds of questions that elicit the appropriate response from the other person.

For example, a lawyer might start with, "What do you want to accomplish by hiring me?" Or "What are you trying to accomplish?"

A financial advisor might inquire, "What do you want a financial plan (or estate plan) to do for you?" Or "What do you want to get from a financial plan?"

A consultant or coach might ask, "What problem are you trying to solve?" Or "What would you like to get by working with me?"

No matter what the other person answers, ask for greater understanding. For instance, you might ask, "How do you mean that, exactly?" They will answer at a deeper emotional level. And then, you ask, "What else do you want?" Keep asking, "What else?" until they say, "That's about it."

Remember, the entire list of things they want must come from them—not you.

Step 3: The Conversation For Value

As with the conversation for possibility, the conversation for value must also come from the prospective client. You say, "Let's suppose that I can help you make all of the things on your list happen. What would the value of that be, in real terms, in your life?"

Be prepared for them to say, "I don't know."

"I don't know" is a default answer most people give. Here is where it comes from. When you are in elementary school, you are excited to answer questions from the teacher. Kids raise their hands and wave their arms vigorously: "Call on me! Call on me!" Until one day you raise your hand and are called upon, and you give the wrong answer. Maybe it's a silly one. The class laughs at you. You are embarrassed and mortified.

Right then and there, you make up your mind that you are never going to do that again. From that moment on, when you are called upon, you answer, "I don't know." Because the class period is thirty to forty-five minutes long, the teacher moves on to someone else to find the answer. "I don't know" worked; it got you off the hook. Furthermore, it gets reinforced and becomes your default answer in life.

In the enrollment process, do not accept "I don't know."

Simply say, "I realize that it's not an easy question. However, think about it. What would it be worth to you?"

The person may say, "A lot." Be prepared for fuzzy, vague, general answers. You must stay focused on getting a real number that represents what the person thinks the value of your product or service would be. Do not browbeat or become aggressive; hang in there and get an answer. It will help you when it's time to discuss your fee.

Step 4: The Conversation For Opportunity

Now you get to talk about your program or service. You can be more focused than you have ever been. You can tailor what you have to say based on what the potential client is looking for. This is not meant to be manipulative in any way. If your service is not what the person is looking for, simply say so and refer them to someone else and move on. You just saved a lot of time and trouble. However, if you are a good fit, then you can speak about your service in a very focused way. You will want to hone your talk to fifteen minutes or less.

Explain how your service works (the elements and the logistics). Don't overdo it. Remember, less is more.

Step 5: The Conversation For Action

No matter how smoothly the rest of the process goes, you still must ask for the business. Coauthor David usually says, "I'm not a great salesperson. I only have one question, and I usually tell you when it's coming—pretty soon. First, do you have any questions?"

Answer any questions they might have. David's favorite question is, "On a scale of one to ten, where one means you never want to see me again and ten means you are ready to start tomorrow, where are you? What will it take to get to ten?"

Or you could also simply ask, "Does this make sense? Are you ready to proceed?" Another option: "Here's the next step; when do you want to start?"

The Five Questions You Must Answer
By Mark LeBlanc, CSP, CPAE

When it comes to your prospective client, they typically have five essential questions on their mind. They may or may not ask them upfront. It is wise never to assume you have all bases covered simply because a person has a problem, and you have the solution. Answering these five questions can spell the difference between a short engagement, a relationship for life, and how often they get the word out about your program, products, presentations, and services.

If you were to look at my roster of active and past clients, as well as where I aim my marketing efforts, you will see common threads weave between them all. When you are clear about the profile of your perfect-fit client, these five questions become much easier to answer. The bonus is your opportunity to be known in a sliver of the marketplace.

The five questions include:

1. What do you do?
2. How do you do it?
3. Why should I buy from you?
4. What are you really all about?
5. What can I expect if I work with you?

Here are my answers as a lighthouse guide to spark your creativity and start your brainstorming process. Please note these are simple answers to simple questions. However, simplicity is seldom easy to get. Resist the temptation to add more or impress others. Letting your ego get between you and your prospective client often results in delaying a decision or a "no" decision.

1. What do you do?

   I work with people who want to start a business and small business owners who want to grow their business.

   (My coaching Defining Statement.)

2. How do you do it?

   Three ways. First, I work one on one with independent and practice professionals who want to create extreme focus and put more money in their pocket as a business owner. As a professional speaker, I conduct presentations on how to generate momentum and nine best practices for true business growth. Third, I have a lineup of tools and materials that support the learning process and help people put ideas into action.

3. Why should I work with you?

   There are three reasons people choose to work with me or have me speak at their meeting or event: knowledge, skills, and relationships. I will provide you with what you need to know in order to grow your business. I will identify certain skills and help sharpen those skills as a business owner.

   Last, but not least, I will show you how to build better relationships with your prospects and your clients.

4. What are you really all about?

   When I work with or speak to an audience, I zero in on four things: direction, identity, marketing, and benchmarking. I want to make sure you are positioned properly and heading in the right direction. Next, I will help you create an identity that supports you in the marketing process.

   From a marketing perspective, I want to make sure you are attracting more prospects and getting your phone to ring. Once you are focused and on track, we will establish certain benchmarks to keep you on track instead of going off on a tangent disguised as an opportunity.

5. What can I expect from working with you?

   Note*: you could tailor this answer to results or deliverables.*

   More focus. More prospects. More referrals. More business.

> *Bottom line, my clients often share they are more focused on a daily basis, able to attract more prospects, stimulate more referrals and ultimately, create a path and a plan for generating more business.*

It took a number of years to reach this level of clarity, succinctness, and authenticity. It reminds me of the quote by Michael Eisner, former chief executive officer of Disney.

According to Eisner, when an idea cannot be articulated simply, crisply, and accessibly, there is usually something wrong with it. He will share that when he hears a good idea, it has an effect on his mind and body. He feels it in his stomach, in his throat and/or on his skin. It becomes a litmus test or instant truth detector test.

Take your time, work diligently and deliberately to craft your answers to these five questions. Learning is never out for the pro. In time and with usage, you will edit answers along the way.

When you are able to answer them simply, crisply, and accessibly, you will have a greater likelihood of enrolling your client, setting the stage for a successful relationship, and getting more referrals. Your proposals, or what I refer to as a discussion document, are more likely to get accepted with less negotiation and seldom a fee reduction.

Beverly
By David Goldman

The year was 1998 and the place was Pittsburgh, PA. Beverly, who sold radio advertising, was struggling. Out of fifteen sales reps, she ranked number fifteen and was a mile away from the top fourteen. Ready to quit, she hired me because she didn't want to quit as a loser; she wanted to be, at least, in the top ten. She signed on for a ninety-day agreement.

Beverly had no trouble getting a meeting. However, she thought she was selling advertising and proceeded to tell the customer everything her program could do for them. The result was no sale. I worked with her on two main concepts: figuring out what the customer really wanted and getting the customer to tell her.

It wasn't easy at first. Beverly had to unlearn everything the company had trained her to do and focus on providing what the client really wanted, which was more customers and more revenue. Nobody wants advertising; they want what advertising can provide for them. Instead of talking about the tool, Beverly began talking about the dream.

The attraction phase conversation helped her focus and attract her ideal markets. The enrollment process helped her concentrate on getting the customer to tell her what they wanted. In six months, working mostly with restaurants, Beverly was number one in new sales and eventually became number three overall out of fifteen. She was kind enough to attribute her success to her shift in mindset and using the Goldman Enrollment Process.

Jonathan
by David Goldman

The year was 2006. Jonathan, a successful attorney in Pittsburgh, PA, was billing $500,000 per year and collecting $250,000 per year. He hired me for two ninety-day agreements to increase his revenue and narrow the gap in collections. Jonathan was very good at what he did, but like most attorneys, he communicated based on his own perspective and wanted the client to understand the process and the payment schedule.

With the Goldman Enrollment Process, he shifted his mindset from himself to the client and what they wanted. Then, all he had to do was explain that he could help make that happen.

It wasn't easy at first. Years of training and experience are hard to shift. In addition, Jonathan's method was working. Billing a half million dollars per year isn't bad, and you can live very comfortably in Pittsburgh on $250,000 per year.

Finally, Jonathan started implementing the enrollment process. He began spending more time listening to what the client wanted and less time expressing what he was going to do. When the client felt like Jonathan understood the situation, realized what they really wanted, and then described how he could help them achieve it, his engagement ratio increased. In fact, it doubled his income from $500,000 to just under $1,000,000. At my suggestion, when Jonathan explained that his fee was really a small percentage of what the client was saving in estate taxes and fees, his collections more than tripled to $950,000.

The shift in mindset from egocentric to client-centric makes all the difference. It worked for Jonathan, and it can work for you.

Where Failure Lurks

There are many reasons why professionals fail at enrollment but it's never due to a lack of commitment.

All professionals are committed to making something great happen. That means for yourself, your family, your clients, and your audiences. You also have conviction. You believe you have something inside of you that can ultimately make a difference and have more impact and influence on the people you serve best.

But where we fall down on the job is a lack of clarity, a lack of congruency, or a lack of consistency. The clearer, more congruent, and more consistent you are, the better your results will be and the more successful you will be.

Measuring Your Meaningful Conversations
By Mark LeBlanc, CSP, CPAE

The litmus test for knowing if your marketing plan is working, is whether or not you are hitting your benchmark of the number of meaningful conversations every thirty days.

For my work, that number is eight meaningful conversations every thirty days. If I hit that number, I know my mix of marketing strategies is paying off. I can hit my target numbers with fewer conversations, however I may be at risk of becoming complacent or inconsistent with implementing my strategies.

What will your benchmark be? The true measure of your business development attraction efforts is whether or not you are hitting that number. The number of meaningful conversations is an important result, but you do not control results. You only control the activities that lead to a result.

The danger in the attraction phase is prematurely enrolling. You do not start the enrolling conversation until the other person clearly raises their hand for it.

The Next Step

After these steps, the enrollment conversation shifts. Now you are ready for the decision phase conversation, which is the focus of the next chapter.

5

THE DECISION PHASE

As you just learned, step five of the enrollment process is the conversation for action, or maybe call to action if you wish.

If you find that a lot of your potential clients or your proposals are going into a black hole, you might have weak decision-phase conversations.

Sometimes you might do everything right in the attraction phase, but you blow it in the meaningful conversation. Sometimes you might have a great meaningful conversation, but your decision-phase conversation is weak. You might need more practice with these conversations, so that you don't fall down on the job.

The goal of the decision phase is to have people agree to work with you, if aspects like fees and timing work out. You might ask an enrolling question like, "If the financial aspects meet your approval, does this sound like the right approach to you?" or "Does this make sense?" or "Are you ready to start?"

If you get an affirmative answer, you can move to the agreement phase covered in the next chapter.

Mastering The Art Of The Decision Phase
By Mark LeBlanc, CSP, CPAE

Asking for the business is a crucial step in the enrollment process. How you do it is as important as when you ask the question. Ask too early in the process and you sound like a salesperson. Asking too late or failing to ask is akin to malpractice in the pursuit of your potential.

It's true that too many professionals secretly hope for a prospect to say, "Yes, I want to work with you, and is it possible to pay you upfront and in full?" The reason for wanting this to occur is we do not have to ask for the order, and it saves us from talking about money and the terms of the sale.

After you get the ear of your prospect in the attraction phase and if you build your case well in your meaningful conversation, it is your right and responsibility as a true resource to create the moment for you to get one of three answers:

Yes, I would like to work with you,
No, I do not think it is a fit for us to work together, or
Yes, and we may need to move our start date for a specific reason.

I built a successful, small printing company over a ten-year period and sold it to pursue my dream of being a professional speaker. Some would have considered me successful at an early age. After I sold my business, I was clear about what I wanted and that was to be a professional speaker.

I struggled terribly in my first twelve months. In fact, I did not make a sale or earn a nickel in my first year. It was a goal I had not remembered setting.

I started year two with a light calendar and little confidence. Somehow by accident I picked up a few business coaching clients. The momentum wheel started to turn, albeit slowly. I read a book titled, *Marketing to The Affluent,* by Stanley Thomas, PhD. The only pearl of wisdom I remember reading was the difference between an OSP (ordinary sales professional) and an ESP (extraordinary sales professional). The crucial difference was an ESP had the courage to ask for the sale.

Armed with this single piece of wisdom, I found myself having lunch with another professional who was interested in hiring me to be his business coach. He was incredibly talented and seriously lacked any sense of business acumen. He kept asking questions and I was getting frustrated. Finally, when he took a breath, I blurted out, "Have I made sense? Would you like to work with me?"

He looked at me and said, "Yes, I would like to work with you. How do we get started?"

Professionals are fearful of asking the question for a number of reasons. One, the fear of rejection is a common reason. Second, a lack of confidence might be the number two reason. The third reason might be as simple as not knowing how to ask for the sale to happen.

Note in my illustration above how I asked two specific questions.

The first was a clarification question, "Have I made sense?" Your clarification question could sound different with different types of services. Our goals are to find out if we are making sense, if we are a good fit and if we have satisfied all of their questions.

The second question is designed to get a simple yes or a kind no. I want to find out at the conclusion of our meaningful conversation if we are on the same page. When you navigate the decision phase well, you will start working with your clients sooner than later. You will prevent opportunities or proposals from languishing in your pipeline. I prefer to get a "no" sooner rather than later, versus hanging on to bad- or wrong-fit opportunities and relationships.

My mother, Lois, built a successful real estate company over a ten-year period. It was the decade after my father had a massive stroke at the age of sixty-one. She did it while she was caring for my father and had significant health challenges of her own, including dialysis and an eventual kidney transplant. When she was asked how she did it with so many commitments, challenges, and obligations on her plate, she simply replied, "If a prospect is not interested in what I have to offer, I simply move on to the next one." My mother mastered the art of the decision phase.

Ask and you will succeed.

6

THE AGREEMENT PHASE

You would love Mary (true story, name changed for privacy). She is a family law attorney in Southern California who really cares about families that go through divorce.

At one point Mary worked part-time as an attorney and was the victim of unexpected misfortune. Her husband left her, and she had to be the sole financial supporter of her two boys.

"I need to double my revenue in one year," Mary related to coauthor Henry, "and all that stuff you teach about generating leads won't work for me. Imagine if I put on a public seminar and the husband walked in one door and the wife came in the other. We might have a divorce right there. Also, unlike your other clients, people come to me for free consulting."

Henry just smiled at the free consulting comment. All professionals get milked for free advice, if they allow it.

"I want you to do two action items," Henry said to Mary. "One, raise your rates from $250 an hour but in 20 percent increments. Practice in a mirror saying: 'My fee is $300 an hour.' When you believe it, raise it to $360 an hour."

"I don't know if I can do that," said Mary. Henry assured her she could.

In fact, clients started to say they were glad they found a $360-an-hour attorney, because they didn't want one of those "$250-an-hour attorneys" handling their divorce.

Henry advised Mary the next step was to offer two-person, twenty-minute seminars at no cost if both the husband and wife would attend.

When Mary's attraction phase work generated phone calls to her assistant, she used the following script:

> *Thank you for asking to speak with Mary. Mary offers two options. If you want to speak with her, she charges $360 an hour. We take your credit card info when you arrive. Most people can get their questions answered in sixty to ninety minutes. We charge the card when you are done with your meeting. Or, as an option, Mary will give you a private, no-cost, twenty-minute seminar on divorce in California, if you and your spouse are willing to attend together. She will explain your options for litigation, mediation, and collaboration. Many people are surprised to find litigation is ten times more expensive and has some unpleasant side effects.*

People made a choice. Mary started to receive $360 an hour for her meaningful conversations with mates who wanted to talk to her alone. "If they want me to fight for them and their children, I am happy to do that," said Mary. She was amazed where some of her clients found the money, but find it they did.

For those mates who would come for the seminar, they found out a wealth of information about mediation and collaboration options.

"After doing the seminars for a time, I could predict if the couple was going to reconcile or divorce based on where they decided to sit in the conference room," said Mary. "I gave them a pre-seminar questionnaire. If they both checked the box saying they would consider reconciliation, I gave them a list of three marriage counselors they might want to talk to."

That is how Mary doubled her revenue in a year through better enrollment conversations.

The Agreement Phase

The agreement phase is where you get into fees, options, and terms. The following checklist approach works well:

- What are my options?
- How much is each option?
- What are the terms?
- What are the payment options?
- Who will serve me?
- When will we start and finish?
- What is the scope of the work?
- Where will the work be done?
- What are the expected results?
- What metrics determine success?

The No-Brainer Agreement Versus The Full Agreement

A decision to make during the agreement phase is whether to offer a full scope of work or a no-brainer agreement. A no-brainer agreement is designed to get an easy yes from the potential client.

An executive management coach, Larry (true story, name changed to maintain confidentiality) was diligent in studying the ins and outs of client enrollment. When Larry gets to the agreement phase of the conversation, he might spell out a scope of work that would be $15,000 for a year. But then he tells the potential client, "But I don't see that for you."

Instead, Larry will tell the person that a two-month 360-degree assessment is more in order. This will cost $2,600 and can just be put on a credit card. During this process, he will interview a client and his executive team. The assessments will help the client determine the true scope of work based on the consensus of the team.

One client said to Larry, "This is music to my ears. You are the eighth executive coach I have talked with, and you are the only one to offer me this easy-to-handle assessment step."

He gave his credit card information, and the two-month engagement began. After working with Larry for two months, the client felt great about the scope and the price and happily signed the agreement document. He was so pleased with the enrollment process he referred other executives to talk to Larry.

This is not a manipulation mind game you are playing with people. This is a way of providing value and helping them get started in a small way.

The Pinpoint Offer

The three coauthors of this book will sometimes offer clients one or two ninety-minute Pinpoint coaching conversations.

Most professionals want to market and provide the full meal deal, or the big-ticket program or a premium package. The traditional thinking was this approach would automatically lead to right- and perfect-fit clients, as well as more money.

One day, Mark came up with an idea that ended up working better than he could have imagined. After losing another opportunity and in a moment of frustration, he realized he could be very helpful to a client if they needed to address a specific business development issue or challenge.

When the next person asked him how he worked with people and when he was in the agreement phase, he shared he could work with people in a variety of ways. He added his goal was to meet the best of what his clients needed and wanted at any stage of their development.

If someone had a specific issue or problem to solve, it might be possible to figure it out in two ninety-minute Pinpoint conversations, i.e., a coaching step. If someone needed more of a makeover or overhaul for their business, it might be better to invest in a ninety-day or five-month coaching engagement. After either a coaching step or coaching engagement, if the fit was right and it made sense to consider a coaching relationship, those options could be explored at the conclusion of that engagement.

The key to Mark's success was positioning the Pinpoint as ninety minutes versus a per hour fee and branding it with the term Pinpoint. It implied focus and a laser-like concentration on a specific challenge or topic.

Imagine if you have an easy or easier entry point to how you worked with your clients. Depending on what you charge per hour, your Pinpoint fee might be as low as $165 to $425 per Pinpoint. You get to choose between a no-brainer fee, or it could be a Goldilocks fee, i.e., not too high or not too low, just right. For many years, Mark billed $365 per Pinpoint. As a result, he began working with more clients and many turned into long-term relationships, resulting in tens of thousands of dollars.

When David added this option to his menu, the results were staggering.

There are two benefits to this offering:

1. The client gets to experience you and your method before engaging in the full program.
2. The client may only want/need a piece of the puzzle and can get that piece handled in ninety minutes or two ninety-minute Pinpoint conversations.

Consider offering a smaller, easier way to work with you. It could make the first decision easier and seed the opportunity for a long-term relationship. It just might work better than you imagine.

Creating The Agreement Document

An agreement document needs to be created and signed by the client. The authors of this book are not attorneys, and we are not going to provide legal advice. The authors do read textbooks on the subject and hire attorneys to help create their documents.

If you think our attorneys made us include that caveat in this book, you would be correct. With that disclaimer out of the way, we can cover some agreement document items in the spirit of education, not providing legal advice. (Please see the copyright page of this book for more details on our disclaimer.)

Here is a checklist of items to consider in your agreements:

- ✓ **Time Period of the Agreement.** What time period is covered? There should be a start and end date.
- ✓ **The Parties to the Agreement.** What are the official names and addresses of the professional and the client?
- ✓ **The Financial Consideration of the Agreement.** Recap of fees and hourly rates, how expenses are handled, and payment options (check, credit card, PayPal, Square, or other means).
- ✓ **Scope of the Agreement.** Recap of what you will do and what is out of scope. There needs to be a meeting of the minds.
- ✓ **Confidentiality Obligations.** Agreement to hold confidential information in confidence in accordance with the terms of the agreement.
- ✓ **Non-Use of Confidential Information.** Agreement to use confidential information solely in accordance with the terms of the agreement.
- ✓ **Definition of Confidential Information.** "Confidential information" shall include all information, written or

oral, disclosed or made available directly or indirectly, through any means of communication or observation.

✓ **Force Majeure.** Obligations shall be extended by a period equal to a force majeure (forces beyond the control of the professional that prevent the professional from meeting the obligations).

✓ **Governing Law.** We ask for the right to do whatever it takes to make you satisfied. If you are not liking our service, please inform us so we can have candid conversations about making you happy. Regardless of where the client lives, this agreement shall be

_____. If any dispute shall arise regarding this agreement, the client and professional shall try to resolve such dispute through collaboration, then through mediation, and if that fails, through binding private arbitration. Our practice is based on satisfied clients, so we hope it never comes to this. Our expectation is you will give us the right and privilege of making you happy.

✓ **Signatures.** This does not necessarily have to be handled the old-fashioned way with quill pen to parchment. There are evolving ways to make it easy on the client with email.

What Comes Next?

The enrollment process is done at this point. You have a signed agreement and money in the bank so you can proceed to help the client solve their problem.

But wait, there is more.

You want referrals. If you are not getting referrals, it might be a clue that you are weak in the agreement phase. To refer people to you, the client must feel good about how the agreement phase was handled. This will be further examined in the next chapter.

7

REFERRALS

There are many professionals who are afraid to ask for referrals. However, you don't have to be afraid.

Let's address a common concern among professionals: the fear of asking for referrals. It's a truism that if you don't ask, you rarely receive. Yet, asking for referrals doesn't have to be intimidating. In fact, we ask our friends for recommendations all the time:

- "Where is a good Chinese restaurant?"
- "We have a leak in our bathroom. Do you know a good plumber?"
- "Where did you buy your last car, and was it a good experience?"

So, why do we hesitate to ask our clients for referrals? Why do we often feel uneasy about it? Perhaps it's because we were never taught how to do it effectively. Or maybe we were taught to ask the wrong questions. It could be that we simply don't know what to say. One thing is certain: we don't want to jeopardize our existing client relationships by coming across as pushy or imposing.

When we do a clumsy job of asking, our clients feel awkward, and their response is often, "Nobody comes to mind." This awkwardness on both sides can lead us to stop asking, or avoid it altogether.

Referrals are too valuable to leave to chance. Up to half of your high-paying clients could come from referrals. So, don't let fear hold you back as you seek them out.

There are specific times when the likelihood of receiving a referral is at its peak. However, keep in mind that asking for a referral involves making a withdrawal from the emotional bank account with your client. Have you built up enough of a balance to earn the right to make such a request? If not, you risk depleting that emotional bank account permanently.

Consider this perspective: To ask for a referral, you must have earned enough trust and goodwill in your client relationship to make the withdrawal without damaging it. One way to increase this balance is by building an authentic, long-term relationship.

As you gain the trust of others, you'll see your emotional bank account balance grow. When you have sufficient balance, you can make a withdrawal without risking the account's closure. Done correctly, asking for a referral can even increase that balance.

Another method to boost your account balance, beyond the usual relationship-building, is through follow-up. Ensure that your product or service continues to meet expectations and that your clients are satisfied with their decision. This is an opportune moment to request a referral, as your clients are reminded of the value you provide.

Here's a hard truth: Relying solely on delivering excellent work does not guarantee referrals. You can excel in your field, achieve desired results, satisfy your clients, and still not receive a single referral.

The secret to stimulating referrals or introductions lies in a three-fold approach:

1. Deliver results consistently.
2. Maintain a strong and consistent agreement phase process.
3. Be open to asking for referrals or introductions to people within your client's network.

If you find that you're not receiving many referrals, it's a signal to fine-tune your agreement phase. When clients enjoy the experience of working with you, they are more likely to reward you with referrals.

Enroll On!
By Mark LeBlanc, CSP, CPAE

Here are solid referral action steps you can take:

Whip your CRM into shape first. Digitize your outreach with a CRM program like Nimble. This is a simple, smart CRM for Office 365 and G-suite teams. You can automatically combine contacts, social media connections, inboxes, and calendar appointments. Some of its clients include GoDaddy, Coldwell Banker, and Upwork. This app allows you to tag a contact multiple times so you can easily segment your relationships by profit center and by type within a profit center. Understand the difference between an advocate or an affiliate relationship and tag accordingly.

Build a list of (up to) twenty-five advocates. Advocates are champions of you and your business who give you referrals for no monetary consideration. Advocates believe in you. An advocate likes to tell people they do not receive any compensation for referring you; they just want the person to be well cared for. To make the advocate list there must be evidence of referring business to you. You want to contact them on a regular basis, and more than twenty-five can become unwieldy. There is nothing wrong with giving small gifts to advocates to show your appreciation, but it cannot be a quid pro quo for every referral or every referral that becomes a client.

Build a list of (up to) twenty-five affiliates. Affiliates are people who will recommend you and expect a financial reward. To make the list they must agree to be willing to refer you for a fee. Typically, this might be in the form of a percentage, with 10 percent being a typical fee, but this will vary by industry. In certain professions, a referral fee is limited or not allowed in any manner. While not mandatory, you are encouraged to draft a letter of understanding so both parties are on the same page regarding your relationship and opportunities for profit.

Decide who you will be an advocate or an affiliate for. As you network, identify people who might make great referral sources. Start with this opener: "If you would be open to a conversation about being referral partners, that would be greatly appreciated." Starting with the word *if* is like a soft knock on the door.

Develop a top-of-mind approach to staying in contact. It is your job to remind them that you exist. Use a variety of means—use email, texting, LinkedIn messages, Facebook messenger, and your phone. Be respectful of their time and keep your expectations to a minimum.

When your key relationships know and can repeat your defining statement, watch your referrals go up!

My world changed forever the day I stumbled upon, or was divinely guided, to a new way to introduce myself at a networking meeting. In my book *Defining You: How Smart Professionals Craft the Answers to: Who Are You? What Do You Do? How Can You Help Me?*[10] I share the concept of the defining statement. Your defining statement is a simple answer to a simple question: what do you do, and who do you do it for? If your defining statement is conversational, you will use it and say it in the marketplace. If it is simple, your advocates will use it as well.

Give if you want to get. If you want to receive referrals, you need to give referrals. Let the law of reciprocity work in your favor. A place to start is to reach out and give specific recommendations on LinkedIn. Be honest and specific. You will be surprised at how many people will return the favor.

Snail mail them little gifts to remind them you appreciate them. Coauthor Henry DeVries will send packets of seeds, baseball cards, unusual paper clips, multicolored Post-it notes, and other items he finds at dollar stores. Include a note expressing your gratitude. Many referral sources say they look forward to the lumpy envelopes that Henry will send on a regular basis.

Be ready with an email response. Chance favors the prepared. When someone sends a referral by email, Henry is ready with a preset response loaded into his signature files in MS Outlook. He will send the email to the referrer and the referral. He thanks the referrer for the introduction, and formally introduces himself in seven sentences and provides a link to his calendar for a no-cost strategy call.

Offer up a template for an email they can send out about you. In mine, I mention the relationship and why they might want to get in touch with me. I make it easy for my advocates and affiliates to pass along my information.

Close the loop. Do your utmost to close the loop with the referrer to tell them what happened and that you appreciate the referral.

David Goldman On Referrals

Most professionals have never been taught how to get referrals. Those who have are taught to ask the wrong question. They are taught to ask, "Who do you know who needs my product or service?"

The client answers, "Nobody comes to mind." Of course, nobody comes to mind. People are not walking around or sitting around thinking about how they can help you. Even when they are open to making an introduction, it never hurts to help them think of people who might be a good fit for you.

The question makes the other person uncomfortable and therefore it makes you uncomfortable. That's why people stop asking for referrals. Not only do you not want your client to be uncomfortable, *but you also don't* want to be uncomfortable.

The David Goldman Service Survey changes the question. You aren't asking who needs your service. (They don't know because we don't talk about those things with one another.) You are finding out what they consider to be "good" service and then you are asking who else in their life believes in service the way they do.

It changes the answer from "nobody" to "everybody." Most people do business with people or hang around people who believe in service the same way they do.

Condense the universe (get them to think of a specific group), ask the service question, and take names and numbers. The David Goldman Service Survey follows:

David Goldman's Service Survey

Question #1—What is "good service"? or how do you define "good service"?

No matter how the person answers, you ask, "How do you mean that, exactly?" Then after that response you ask, "What else?" until they say, "That's about it."

Question #2—What do you like about the service you're getting now? (Don't allow your ego to get overblown.)

Repeat response strategy from question one. Ask: "And how do you mean *that*?" Then after that response you ask, "What else?" until they say, "That's about it."

Question #3—What's missing from the service you're getting now? In other words, what's not present that if it *were* present, it would make a difference? (Don't get defensive or begin explaining yourself.)

Once again repeat response strategy from question one. Ask: "Meaning?" Then, after that response you ask, "What else?" until they say, "That's about it."

Then, you transition to having them think about a close circle of people (customers, vendors, friends, etc.) and ask, "How many of them believe in service the way you do?"

Get names, emails, and phone numbers.

8

SUMMING IT UP

No prospective client wants to be sold, but they are looking for a solution to their problem. You enroll someone into the possibility that your product or service is for them. The process involves four phases.

1. **During the attraction phase, the objective is to get people to ask for a conversation about how you could help them.** No more "spray and pray" business development. Put into place a proactive process for getting people to raise their hand and request further conversation. There are several proven strategies to generate attraction phase conversations. These include speaking, writing, networking, podcasting, and volunteering.

2. **During the meaningful conversation phase, there are four major steps.** 1) The Background of Relationship - establishing rapport. 2) The Conversation for Possibility - the potential client tells you what they want. 3) The Conversation for Value - the potential client tells you what the value would be to get what they want. 4) The Conversation for Opportunity - you get to describe your service and how it works.

3. **During the decision phase, there is a call to action.** No matter how smoothly the rest of the process goes, you still must ask for the business. Answer any questions the person might have. A good question might be, "On a scale of one to ten, where one means you never want to see me again and ten means you are ready to start tomorrow, where are you? What will it take to get to ten?"

4. **Finally, during the agreement phase, you must nail down the details.** The enrollment process is not done until there is a signed agreement and money has exchanged hands. Your ability to generate referrals will depend on how your new clients feel emotionally about this part of the process.

Jack And Steven
By David Goldman

The year was 2019. Jack and Steven were young associates working for an independent financial planning firm in Pittsburgh, PA. Most training involves operational procedures, compliance, and how products work. Very little is done regarding how to develop target markets and how to have conversations that produce results (in other words, get clients). Even when using sales training, it often involves learning how to close a sale; not develop a relationship. I was referred to both Jack and Steven by a long-term client. After much eye rolling and skepticism, they agreed to hire me to help increase their production and revenue.

It wasn't easy at first. There was much to unlearn, and they both had to spend time and effort on foundational shifts in mindset. For example, the idea of a perfect-fit client was brand new to them. Some prospective clients were better suited than others. In other words, they might not want every person who was willing to buy from them. In addition, developing a strong, simple, defining statement proved valuable as an answer to the question, "What do you do?" Slowly but surely, they became focused on attracting the right person, not just making a sale.

The most impactful concept involved using the Goldman Enrollment Process. For the first time, Jack and Steven had a format to use when conducting an initial meeting that focused on the client and what they wanted. It gave Jack and Steven a strategy they could follow and allowed them the freedom to enroll right-fit clients instead of just making sales. Their results soared.

After working with me for one year, Jack's production increased 57 percent and Steven's increased 122 percent. Both attributed the results to being more comfortable with the conversations in the phases of attraction and enroll-ment (meaningful conversation). Even through the pan-demic and as of this writing, they continue to thrive and produce outrageous results.

In short, the enrollment process works. The four phases of engagement with prospective clients also work. It has worked in these stories. It has worked in many other examples. It can work for you.

There is a bonus phase, and that is getting referrals. Remember, you control the enrollment process, but the other person provides the answers. When done correctly, the potential client feels in control of the entire enrollment process. That feeling is critical to gaining referrals. A positive emotional feeling will generate referrals. You want people to feel like you really understand them, and they are seen and heard. They also must feel you have a proven process for solving problems like theirs. Then, they will be happy to refer you. To be successful with referrals, you need to cultivate advocates (your cheerleaders) and where appropriate, affiliates (your partners).

BONUS CHAPTER

HOW TO NEGOTIATE SPEAKING FEES

By Mark LeBlanc, CSP, CPAE

O ver the course of time, I've given over one thousand paid presentations. I have tried enrolling speaking clients by quoting fees every which way: up and down and sideways. I've made every mistake in the book and learned from those mistakes. In fact, I've made some mistakes multiple times.

Quite frankly, trusted advisors have the opportunity to earn really well for a one-hour keynote speech or a three-hour workshop. We all grow up with different attitudes, habits, beliefs, behaviors, and values around money. While you might waive your fee for marketing purposes, there is an opportunity for you to command top dollar for sharing your expertise in a presentation. Getting paid to speak may not be your goal, however it may make sense to prepare yourself for these types of opportunities.

Commanding higher speaking fees is not brain surgery, although you will need to study and practice a new way of approaching the agreement phase of the process.

The Biggest Fee Mistake Most Speakers Make

Most speakers come out of the gate and create a fee schedule based on two variables. The first variable is geography. Where is the presentation? If it's in your town, you charge X. If it's out of town, you might charge an extra $1,000 or whatever you feel needs to be added for travel time.

The second variable is the length of the presentation. For example, a keynote presentation is X, up to half a day is more, and up to a full day is even more.

While I do not consider myself a contrarian, I do not think and approach my speaking fees based on geography and length of a presentation.

In fact, my approach is to think like an artist but act like a business owner. It's important to step back and be reminded that there are four phases to the marketing and selling process.

The Four Phases Applied To Speaking Fees

As noted earlier, the first phase is the attraction phase, the second phase is the meaningful conversation phase, the third phase is the decision phase, and the fourth phase is the agreement phase. I've slightly tweaked the goal of each phase to reflect booking speaking gigs.

In the attraction phase, the goal is to get the ear of a potential client or obtain inbound interest, which is an inquiry. That's all we want.

We want that person to raise his or her hand and say, "I want to know more about having you speak at our conference or for our organization." Then we move into a meaningful conversation.

In the meaningful conversation phase, the goal is to get the person to say they want to book you. This is a specific conversation where you are building a case for someone to say, "Yes, we want to book you," or second, "No, I don't think this is a fit," or third, "Yes, this makes sense, but for whatever reason, we need to delay our decision." If you find your economic buyers saying, "We're going to have to think about it and get back to you," it's likely the quality level of your meaningful conversation is wafer-thin or weak.

When I sharpened my skills on having a more meaningful conversation, I came to realize it was as important as improving my presentation and performance skills in front of an audience.

In the decision phase, your goal is to get an answer regarding fit, not the fee. It is the answer to, "Does this make sense? Is it the type of presentation or experience you want for your people?"

Then we move into the agreement phase or scope of the engagement. At first it can appear daunting. In time, you will improve your confidence and create better agreements.

In the agreement phase, the goal is to nail down the specifics. The agreement phase is where you start to talk about fees, scope, variables, terms, steps, contracting, and all of those other items that go into the agreement. Instead of the term proposal, I prefer to call it a discussion document.

Audience Fit Is Key

It is important to combine the four phases with an understanding of audience and organizational fit. There are six different types of fit in the marketplace. On the positive side, there's a perfect-fit, a right-fit, and a good-fit audience. On the negative side, there's a bad-fit, a wrong-fit, and a horrible-fit audience. (See Appendix A)

Never enter into an agreement phase conversation unless it's a good-, right-, or perfect-fit audience. Graciously excuse yourself from bad-fit, wrong-fit, and horrible-fit type audiences.

Here is one factor to take into consideration: the concept of a mixed audience versus a pure audience. In the world of business development, an example of a mixed audience would be a chamber of commerce. Even though it's a business group, it's a mixed audience of different types of businesses from different sectors or industries. A chamber audience or similarly mixed audience could include bankers, managers, small business retail, manufacturing, and services, the arts, antiques, and even the Dairy Queen owner. It's just a mixed audience, usually ending in mixed results or reviews.

A pure group, as I define it, is a gathering of your target audience. A pure group for me is when I'm in front of ninety top producers for Smith Barney, twenty independent consultants, eight hundred real estate agents, two hundred insurance agents, or ninety graphic designers. When you determine who you serve best as a right-target audience, you can aim your efforts to be in front of a pure audience of your best fit.

Other Variables To Consider
Along the way I expanded the list of variables to include:

- Length of presentation
- Type of organization

- Geography
- Expenses
- Type of presentation
- Multiple (same) presentations
- Multiple (other) presentations
- Book sales
- Licensing
- Terms
- Streaming/recording opportunities

Certainly, the type of organization is a factor. Is it a corporation? Is it an association? Is it a nonprofit? Is it a religious organization? Is it an educational organization? Many speakers have different fees for different types of organizations.

And then I thought, "Well, if the type of organization is important, what about the number and type of presentation?" More often than not, I create an agreement to deliver the keynote speech, and a general session the next morning, or the keynote speech and a breakout session, or the keynote speech and two breakout sessions. I might be considered a single, conference breakout session or the same workshop repeated or even multiple breakout sessions on different topics.

Regarding travel expenses, there are some organizations that want to pay you for actual out-of-pocket expenses after the event. Some speaking clients appreciate an inclusive fee. I would ask a potential client, "Would you prefer I bill you after the event for the actual travel expenses or would you prefer include a reasonable estimate for usual and customary travel expenses, so we don't have to worry about that post-event?"

I discovered that seven out of ten, economic buyers wanted a fee that was inclusive of my travel expenses.

It's gotten more complicated because of recording rights and licensing rights. It is common for your client to assume that what they pay you to do your presentation includes the right to record the presentation and for them to own it in perpetuity. I do not know where they got that idea, but it has become a natural assumption that it is usual and customary—and it's not. Licensing, recording, and usage are additional variables that must be taken into consideration long before you arrive at the speaking venue.

Terms of payment are an important variable. Remember PVM, the present value of money. I have negotiated my fee based on being paid upfront in full a year or up to eighteen months in advance if their budget was tighter. Typically, you ask for 50 percent upfront and 50 percent on the speaking date.

We always know in our heart and in our gut if someone is trying to beat us up on our fees, or if there simply isn't a budget for our fees. Will I negotiate a fee agreement? Of course, I will. I am much more likely to negotiate a speaking fee once I clarify the opportunity and the respective variables to the agreement.

I will always listen to how my potential clients communicate with me and what they say to me. By the way, I always, only, and ever want to talk with the economic buyer, never a gatekeeper. It's a little bit more challenging when you're working with trade and professional associations. I understand. When the opportunity presents itself, I will certainly provide information to the gatekeeper or the person who's gathering information. As a standard, I will never negotiate a fee agreement with someone gathering information for a decision maker or speaker selection committee.

For example, let's say you get an email, "Are you available on April 30 in Louisville, Kentucky, and what's your fee?" My email response or better yet, voicemail message will say, "Thank you so much for reaching out. I just wanted to give you a quick call.

"I'm going to respond to your email by _____. Your opportunity sounds like a perfect-fit audience for me and my expertise. I will look forward to hearing from you after you have a chance to review some of my information."

How To Talk About Fee Range

How I address the fee question is really very simple. "Thank you for asking. My fee range is X to 2X." Fee ranges seem to work better as an equation of X to 2X. Your fee range could be $1,000 to $2,000, or $2,500 to $5,000, or $5,000 to $10,000, or $10,000 to $20,000. Never ever, ever, ever is it: "My fee range is about $1,000 to $5,000, or $3,000 to $9,000." Those gaps are too large. When you position your fee range as X to 2X, you will open yourself up to better opportunities and more valuable experiences.

Take careful note of this language because I really want you to practice this. When an organization reaches out, usually in an email, my response is most often, "Thank you for asking. My fee range for my keynote speech, 'Never Be the Same,' is X to 2X. Is that a range you are comfortable with?"

That's exactly how I will either write it in an email or articulate it in a conversation over the phone. To repeat: "Is that a fee range you are comfortable with?" I am looking for or listening for one of three responses:

Number one response: shock. "Oh my God, you charge how much? Oh, we've never paid that much for a speaker." Your fee range might be $100 to $200, and you will still get, "Oh my God, we've never paid a speaker $100 bucks. Are you kidding me?"

Number two response: sounds reasonable. Your right- and perfect-fit organizations will often respond with, "Well, that sounds reasonable. That's where we thought you might land. Mark, what makes the difference?" And that's the response I'm looking for. We don't have a prayer with the shock response. We want to hear, "Well, that sounds reasonable. We've done our research. We've ordered your book, or we've ordered a couple of your books. Let's talk about what makes the difference and determine if you are the right speaker for this event."

Number three response: effusiveness. If they are overly enthusiastic, be wary. "Oh my God, that's it? That's your fee range? Oh, we thought you were $40,000. I mean, everything that our research suggests you're in that league with so and so, and so and so." When I first heard effusiveness, I thought it would be a guaranteed booking. After several times, I began to realize they were simply fishing. With an overly effusive or enthusiastic response, I discovered there was always a reason to delay the decision. These prospects usually ghosted my attempts to reach them again and the opportunities ended up in the black hole.

If the response is shock, I will simply be as respectful and as gracious as I can be. I will let them know I understand and will offer to suggest other speakers that would be open to speaking for their organization.

When I get the reasonable response, they will ask: "What makes the difference or how do you determine where you land as a final fee?"

Word for word here is what I say: "Unlike other speakers who tend to quote a speaking fee based on two variables, the length of the presentation and geography, I've come up with a handful of other variables that can impact your final investment. It doesn't take me long to walk you through those variables and we can figure out what's important to you and what's important to me. We can create a fee agreement that honors both of us."

Then I will say, "Candidly, I'm driven by a single question. That question is, "What will meet the best of what your members or what your audience members need and want?" As I said, it doesn't take me long to walk through these variables. With most inquiries, they've already given me three, four, or five of the variables.

They've told me where it's going to be, what they're looking for, the type of organization, and how many people might be in the audience. I then ask the appropriate questions to fill in a couple of blanks. By the way, I actually have an estimate sheet with these variables that, when I have an opportunity, I pull out and just start making notes. I guess you could call it a lead sheet, but it's an estimate sheet for me to figure out what the right fee would be.

Then I'll just ask them some questions. "Where is it going to be? How many people again? And you want me to come in and give a keynote speech at a three-day conference? Great. Have you booked any other speakers at my level?"

If the answer is effusive, I treat it as I would the potential clients who think my fee range sounds reasonable. But I do not make the mistake of thinking the gig is a done deal.

If this is a perfect-fit or right-fit audience for me, I might say, "Is there an opportunity to maybe come in and do the keynote and maybe a breakout session or a general session the next morning? In fact, several organizations will book me for a keynote. And then they will have me do a presentation, a roll-up-your-sleeves application version of my nine best practices for business development."

When You Are Close But Budget Matters

Sometimes they've given me a hint, "Well, Mark, I know you've got this fee range. Is there any way we can be closer to the lower end of the range?"

Then I say, "Well, certainly. Let's figure that out." And if we can agree on the lower end of the range, great.

But I've had organizations that come to me with a fee that's outside of the low end of my range, and I'm able to get them into my range by having a better meaningful conversation. It is important that you understand there are a lot more variables here than meet the eye. I would encourage you to share your fee range in the attraction phase and wait until the agreement phase to present a final fee. Many professionals have been in situations where you quoted a fee, and a decision maker did not have the budget for it. At that point you need to backpedal and start finding ways to add value. Why not figure out ways to add value by being a better needs analyzer and opportunity finder? Anchor the fee as an investment in the outcome they want for their audience members—not a cost for a body to be put in front of the room to satisfy a need or solve a problem.

There are times I will accept opportunities lower than the low end of my range. There are also times I will end up with a fee more than the higher end of my range based on the conversation and the variables. I might ask how many people are going to be there. They might answer seventy-five.

I might say: "What if I signed seventy-five books in advance and we have them ready to gift to everyone? By the way, I'm coming to Chicago. I've got no need to come back right away on Saturday afternoon. What if I stuck around? If you pick up another night, I'll stay the weekend. Why not allow me the opportunity to hang out with your seventy-five business owners over the course of the weekend?"

All of a sudden you will have people saying, "You mean you do this and this and this, and you would do it all for that fee? Let me make a call and let me see if I can get that approved. I'll call you back."

They are happier paying you more this year than they did last year for the speaker because they got so much more value.

APPENDIX A

SIX KINDS OF CLIENT FIT

Not all prospective clients are created equal. There are six kinds of client fit. Three are positive and above the line, and three are negative and below the line.

The above-the-line fits are:

- Perfect Fit. Everything just clicks when you work with these types of people.
- Right Fit. Not perfect, but excellent.
- Good Fit. Not bad, but not great. You will work with them, but they are not ideal.

And then below-the-line are:

- Bad Fit. Something is just off in the relationship.
- Wrong Fit. You are not right for everybody, and you are definitely wrong for these bodies.
- Horrible Fit. The client from hell. It's a wrong fit that makes it your fault.

Before you try to attract new clients, take a moment to understand who the perfect-, right-, and good-fit clients are for you. Create a profile of your perfect-fit client. This involves more than just the demographics of industry, gender, income, location, and age (just to name a few). This also means the behaviors, opinions, and attitudes your perfect-fit clients demonstrate. The more you understand what you are looking for, the easier it will be to attract this type of person.

On the flip side, understanding what a bad-, wrong-, and horrible-fit client looks like can be extremely helpful. During your interviews the people will give clues to identify themselves. Do not work with people just because they want to be your clients. To avoid future headaches, we suggest being selective by avoiding bad, wrong, and horrible fits as clients.

Judy

By David Goldman

The year was 2010. Judy, a successful executive search professional, knew she could be doing better. In addition, she was the top producer in her office but wasn't getting the recognition she deserved. When Judy hired me, she wanted to make more money and be more independent. I didn't need to teach Judy how to sell. In fact, she could and did teach me a few things. What I did help her see was how to value herself and ask for what she wanted.

She learned the new approach to the attraction phase, and the enrollment process certainly provided a better system for getting perfect-fit clients. However, Judy's real breakthrough was in standing up for herself and renegotiating her agreement so that she made more money per client while also increasing the number of clients. After six months, Judy was still the number one producer and happier than ever.

She continued to work with me and within the next couple years, she partnered with a colleague to start her own operation. Judy continues to use the four phases of attraction, meaningful conversation, decision, and agreement along with the enrollment process to produce results for her clients in her own executive search firm.

APPENDIX B

ACKNOWLEDGMENTS

David Goldman. Most, if not all, lifetime journeys start with your childhood. Mine was good, not perfect but relatively noneventful. First and foremost, I want to thank my parents and my brother for doing, as my mother would say, "The best they could." Along with many teachers in school, they provided the love and the challenges that fueled my love of learning and my search for self-acceptance.

As an adult, I have stood on the shoulders of many great teachers. Jim Rohn, Brian Tracy, Stephen Covey, Kevin Cullen, Don Miguel Ruiz, Bill Gove, Alan Weiss, Jack Canfield, Bob Dunwoody, and Mark LeBlanc have each contributed greatly to my growth and whatever success I may have attained.

A special note about Mark LeBlanc. I have hired him twice as my coach to grow my business. In 1996, he completely shifted my mindset, which provided a quantum leap in my results. A few years ago, I hired him again, and he will be on my team forever. This book wouldn't exist without Mark. In addition, he introduced me to his partner at Indie Books International, Henry DeVries. Of course, Mark and Henry are my co-authors on this book. Thank you both.

A special thank you to Henry, his daughter Devin, and the entire team at Indie Books International. They are amazing people, easy to work with, and this book would not be the same without them.

My children are amazing human beings. They have taught me so much about life, leadership, and love. My son Hank and my daughter Anna are my heroes and continue to inspire me.

Thank you to all of my clients over the years who put their faith and trust in me. I hope that I made a difference in your business and in your life. Please know that I learned as much from you as you may have learned from me.

Last and certainly not least, my girlfriend, partner, and love of my life, Terri Polacheck helped immensely with editing, listening, support, and encouragement.

Henry DeVries. I wish to express gratitude for my many mentors who have recently passed: Professor Glen Broom of San Diego State University, the world's leading public relations scholar, for four decades of mentoring and friendship; *Chino Champion* newspaper publisher Al McCombs, who gave me, at the age of fifteen, my first paying job as a writer; my first coauthor Diane Gage Lofgren, who in 1990 taught me to be a coauthor; and Professor Jack Douglass of UC San Diego, who in 1975 gladly took this teenager straight off a farm under his wing and taught me how to create the career of my dreams.

Also I want to thank the team at Indie Books International, including Mark LeBlanc, Ann LeBlanc, Vikki DeVries, Devin DeVries, Suzanne Hagen, Joni McPherson, Denise Montgomery, Jack DeVries, Don Sevrens, Sally Romoser, Heather Pendley, Taylor Graham, Adrienne Moch, Lisa Lucas, Eric Gudas, Jordan

DeVries, Bill Ramsey, Steve Plummer, and so many others who have helped me create my masterpiece: a business that is the Apple computer of consultant books, making it easy and affordable for every consultant to have more credibility, more impact, and more influence.

To my Heavenly Father, thank you for helping me expand my territory so I can serve more of your children to get what they want in life. Thank you to the hundreds of authors, vendors, and investors who chose Indie Books International.

Mark LeBlanc. I have a deep well of mentors, friends, and clients who have shaped the way I think, make decisions, act, and celebrate my results. These include Robert Rickey, Bob Thorson, Fr. Ken Opat, OSC, Gus Lactaoen, Mike McKinley, Bob Erickson, Dr. Lyman K. (Manny) Steil, Tim Gard, John Blumberg, Francis Bologna, Dr. John Givogre, Henry DeVries, Eleni Kelakos, Terri Langhans, Sherry Coauette, John LeBlanc, Kylie Strem, and so many more.

At twenty-one, when my employer suggested I did not have the work ethic to make it on my own, I vowed to do whatever it would take to be my own boss and make it on my own. I will soon celebrate my fortieth year of entrepreneurial success and achievements and have earned many accolades along the way. Last, but not least, I wish to thank every single professional who trusted me, believed in my work, and attended one of my Achievers Circle business development retreats.

APPENDIX C

ABOUT THE AUTHORS

David Goldman. As founder, owner, and president of Goldman Organization, David elevates and accelerates results for professionals and executives. Since November 1989, he has worked with professionals (accountants, attorneys, financial advisors, and business owners) who want to bring in more business and executives who want to be more effective and move up in their organizations. He consults, coaches, and teaches them to communicate more effectively so they get the results they really want.

David also speaks to groups on various topics that get them to think, take action, and perform at a higher level.

Since 1989, David has clocked more than 25,000 coaching hours helping clients achieve results. For example, a financial advisor reported results of more than $700,000 in additional new revenue over a seven-year period working with David.

As a result of his work, professionals and executives get the four C's: more clarity, more certainty, more confidence, and more control in their communication. That leads to more revenue, more balance, better relationships, and more fulfillment.

On a personal note, since November 1992, David has been the bass/baritone singer in the oldies rock and roll band Magic Moments.

David's first book is *The Road To Happiness – How To Get What You Really Want*.

To reach David, you may email him at david@goldmanorganization.com or call him at 412-377-6200.

Henry DeVries, MBA, APR. Henry is the host of *Agency Rainmaker TV*. He is the CEO of Indie Books International and has ghostwritten or edited more than three hundred business books, including his #1 Amazon sales and marketing best-seller, *How To Close A Deal Like Warren Buffett*. You can read his business development columns for Forbes.com at www.forbes.com/sites/henrydevries. In his book and presentations titled "Persuade With A Story!" he shows thousands of professionals each year how to uncover hidden asset hero stories that communicate trustworthiness in two minutes or less. He earned his MBA from San Diego State University and a certificate in Leading Professional Service Firms from the Harvard Business School.

On a personal note, he is a baseball nut who has visited forty-four major league baseball parks and has three to go before he can touch 'em all. He can be reached at henry@indiebooksintl.com. Learn more about Henry on his LinkedIn page: https://www.linkedin.com/in/henryjdevries/ or by visiting the website for Indie Books International: http://indiebooksintl.com.

Other Books By Henry DeVries:

Self-Marketing Secrets (with Diane Gage)

Pain-Killer Marketing (with Chris Stiehl)

Client Seduction (with Denise Montgomery)

Closing America's Job Gap (with Mary Walshok and Tappan Monroe)

Marketing the Marketers

How to Close a Deal Like Warren Buffett (with Tom Searcy)

Marketing with a Book

Persuade with a Story!

Client Attraction Chain Reaction

Build Your Consulting Practice (with Mark LeBlanc)

Defining You (with Mark LeBlanc and Kathy McAfee)

Persuade With A Case Acceptance Story! (with Penny Reed and Mark LeBlanc)

Persuade With A Digital Content Story! (with Lisa Apolinski)

Rainmaker Confidential (with Scott Love and Mark LeBlanc)

Marketing With A Book For Agency Owners

24 Ways To Get Paid To Speak (with Nona Prather)

Trusted Advisor Confidential (with Craig Lowder)

Mark LeBlanc, **CSP, CPAE.** Mark runs a speaking business based out of Minneapolis, Minnesota. He conducts presentations and creates retreat-type experiences for independent and practice professionals who want to create an extreme sliver of focus and put more money in their pocket. His nationally renowned Achievers Circle business retreat is ideal for professionals who want to develop a path and plan for true business growth.

In fact, he has authored or coauthored five business development books, including his underground bestseller, *Growing Your Business*. He has given over a thousand presentations and conducted over two hundred business retreats. Mark is a past president of the National Speakers Association and was inducted into the Minnesota Speakers Hall of Fame in 2006. He can be reached at Mark@GrowingYourBusiness.com. Learn more about Mark on his LinkedIn page: https://www.linkedin.com/in/speaker-mark-leblanc-89b311/ or his website: www.MarkLeBlanc.com.

Other Books By Mark LeBlanc:

Growing Your Business

Never Be The Same

Build Your Consulting Practice (with Henry DeVries)

Defining You (with Kathy McAfee and Henry DeVries)

Persuade With A Case Acceptance Story! (with Penny Reed and Henry DeVries)

Rainmaker Confidential (with Henry DeVries and Scott Love)

APPENDIX D

SCHEDULE A
"BRINGING IN THE BUSINESS" RETREAT

There is something all professional service firms need right now: *more clients.*

If you would be open to a conversation about a Bringing in the Business Retreat for your firm, please reach out to David Goldman, Henry DeVries, or Mark LeBlanc.

Ideally, retreats take place with a three-hour Thursday afternoon session, a Thursday networking dinner, and then two three-hour sessions and lunch on a Friday. However, they can be tailored to your specific needs and schedule.

There are a few variables that determine the investment for the retreat which we are happy to discuss with you.

The new normal is not normal for a professional service firm; it is more like trying to find clients on a burning platform. For thirty years, the metaphor of a burning platform has symbolized an intense level of urgency for change, but it has never been truer. These are urgent times and to connect with clients and become influential, your professional service firm needs to include storytellers who can attract clients, land accounts, and cement client relationships.

Find out what you need to know and what you need to do to take your firm to the next level. As business development experts, we share best practices around bringing in the business, including insider strategies, steps, and tools for making it happen in the new normal.

These days there is one hidden asset that will set you apart, something nobody else is offering: *your defining stories.* Together, let's mine those hidden asset stories.

APPENDIX E

WORKS REFERENCED AND AUTHORS' NOTES

[1] David Maister, *Managing The Professional Service Firm* (New York: Free Press, 1997).

[2] Tony Allesandra and Phil Wexler, *Non-Manipulative Selling* (New York: Prentice Hall Press, 1987).

[3] Tony Allesandra, *The Platinum Rule* (New York: Warner Business Books, 1998).

[4] Jeff Thull, *Mastering The Complex Sale* (Hoboken, NJ: Wiley, 2nd edition, 2010).

[5] Tom Searcy and Barbara Weaver Smith, *Whale Hunting* (Hoboken, NJ: Wiley, 2008). Coauthor Henry DeVries also cowrote with Searcy *How To Close A Deal Like Warren Buffett* (New York: McGraw-Hill, 2013).

[6] "David Sandler wanted to take control of the sales call, his results, and ultimately, his life. The resulting Sandler Selling System has become the most popular, efficient, and effective way to sell. Sandler teamed up with a clinical psychologist and designed an approach to sales that would break the traditional stereotypes of salespeople. It would focus on mutual respect,

clarity, and qualifying decisions. And finally, it would take the pressure off the salesperson and the prospect, so that both parties can enjoy the process." Source: www.sandler.com.

[7] Mark LeBlanc, Kathy MacAfee, and Henry DeVries, *Defining You* (Oceanside, CA: Indie Books International, 2019).

[8] Jim Horan, *The One Page Business Plan* (Berkeley, CA: The One Page Business Plan Company, 2006).

[9] Mark LeBlanc, Kathy McAfee, and Henry DeVries, *Defining You* (Oceanside, CA: Indie Books International, 2019).

[10] Bryan Gray, Jesse Laffen, Paul Davison, and Mike Rendel. *The Priority Sale* (Oceanside, CA: Indie Books International, 2021).

APPENDIX F

MORE PRAISE FOR THE AUTHORS

"I attended Mark's signature business retreat, The Achiever's Circle. It was the start of a relationship that would create possibilities beyond what I thought possible and build an extraordinarily successful consulting firm. With Mark's highly developed and keen sense of listening for 'what really matters,' he patiently prescribed insights and ideas that transformed my business. We created a strategic playbook and implemented a new business model coming out of the pandemic. He is an exemplary advisor and coach, as well as an extraordinary human being."

Stuart Friedman,
President/Founder,
Progressive Management Associates

"Henry's support and recommendations have added at least $250,000 per year in additional revenues in the past decade."

Barry Deutsch, Founder
Impact Hiring Solutions

"I have had the opportunity to work with David over the last ten years and have found his insight and style to be career changing for me. David's style and guidance have allowed me to reach the top of my career."

Ken Como,
President and CEO, Bill Few Associates

"After my book *Always Forward* was published, my standard keynote fee became $15,000. Henry distills his vast knowledge in marketing through hands-on, straightforward, easy-to-understand lessons that can be applied to generate results."

Bill Wooditch,
president of The Wooditch Company,
author of bestseller *Always Forward*

"Shortly after working with David, I went to a six-figure income for the first time in my life and developed life philosophies that have made for a balanced, happy career and personal life for the past thirty years. Today, I have a seven-figure revenue stream, three offices in two states, and a staff of twelve. I believe in my heart of hearts that David Goldman was the man who gave me many of the tools and the inspiration to be the person I am today."

David L. Hodge, Partner,
Harper & Hodge Wealth Management

"I have had the good fortune of knowing David for over twenty-five years both as a friend and professional. David is a gifted communicator with a deep knowledge and scholarship of salesmanship. The most compelling quality that separates David is his innate ability to perceive and understand the weakness many professionals harbor and never address. His passion to help others succeed is both refreshing and significantly rewarding. For all who desire improvement with their sales process, I highly recommend *Bringing in The Business*, a must-read and study."

James W. Monteverde, CLU, ChFC, AEP,
President and CEO, The Monteverde Group, LLC

"In the last four years, with Henry's help I have written three books and tripled my revenues."

Lisa Apolinski,
digital marketing agency owner of 3 Dog Write

"I met with David Goldman when I was in transition and when I started as a Vistage Chair. In those meetings, David helped me to clarify who would be a perfect fit for me and my group, and what they would want. That helped immensely in my marketing effort. I always learn from David and appreciate his way of looking at things and how he can get me to shift how I look at things. Read this book. Engage and learn from him. You won't be sorry you did."

Kevin Trout, Vistage Peer Advisory Group Chair,
Host, *Three Rivers Leadership* Radio Show and
Podcast, former CEO of Grandview Medical
Resources, Inc.

"In 2018 I started my business, Oral Cancer Consulting, and named my oral cancer screening method, the Cotten Method of Screening, without a clear plan on how to grow my business. I heard Mark LeBlanc speak in January of 2019 on growing your business and having your fun meter on max, I immediately knew I needed to work with Mark! Through the pandemic, my business and gross revenue grew exponentially, with Mark's assistance I signed a 'whale of a contract' as a consultant with my state in late 2020. In 2023, the fifth year with Mark as my business coach, I signed a third contract with the state, spoke in twelve different states to thousands of dental professionals, won a speaking competition, and began the work on my dream collaboration. I am where I am today both professionally and personally because Mark is my business coach."

Susan Cotten,
Owner, Oral Cancer Consulting

"When I first met David Goldman in August of 2021 I did not like the direction my law firm was heading. I was constantly busy and yet not reaping the financial rewards I felt that I should have been.

"In working with David over the past year and a half, he helped me realize the value of the services we provide. David also helped me focus on working with better clients, what his method refers to as a 'good fit' or 'perfect fit.' Prior to meeting David many of my clients were *bad fits* in that they did not appreciate the hard work I was putting in on their case, blamed me for their problems, and worst of all, did not pay their bills. David really helped me eliminate these clients and manage my time better so I could focus on the types of cases and types of clients that I wanted.

"As an attorney who primarily practices in the area of estates, probate, and trusts, David helped me market myself in ways I never thought of before."

Nathan L. Bible, Esq., LLM,
Partner NBMS Law, PC

"I have been working with David since mid-2020, smack in the middle of the pandemic. He's been a great resource and confidant in enabling me to both restore and reinforce confidence in myself and abilities, as well as being a phenomenal sounding board. David has made all the difference in the world for me, at a time when my career needed it the most. He is a great listener and exhibits great balance between confidant and coach. I would recommend David's book to anyone who is looking to *up their game* and be their best self."

Ronald R. Celaschi, President and CEO,
Clearview Federal Credit Union

"The book Henry helped me publish is a tremendous support to my digital marketing agency and has helped us grow to over $2 million in annual revenues."

Thomas Young,
digital marketing agency owner of
Intuitive Websites and author of
Winning the Website War

"I first met Mark at his Achiever's Circle retreat - those three days changed my business and served as a catalyst for me to continue my entrepreneurial journey. At the time, I had no idea how critical working with Mark would be to my success. As 2020 had different plans than anyone envisioned with the pandemic, Mark supported, guided, and motivated me to continue building my new business, and I was able to hit my financial goals in 2020 when so many other similar firms were struggling. Since then, my business has continued to grow and evolve with Mark playing a key role alongside me every step of the way. If you are considering working with Mark, then that means he has made such an invitation to you - do not take that lightly. I encourage you to take advantage of any opportunity to engage with him and have him as your coach and guide."

Scott Cantrell,
Founder, Smart Solutions Media

"The first book Henry helped me publish has been instrumental in securing 23 clients and $942,000 in personal income, along with a six-year lead conversion rate of 88 percent."

Craig Lowder,
founding principal of Smooth Selling
Forever sales consultancy,
author of *Trusted Advisor Confidential*

"Working with Mark LeBlanc over the past year and a half has been a transformative experience for us. His unwavering belief in our potential and his commitment to our success have been nothing short of inspiring. During a year when we were laser-focused on a significant goal, Mark's support was a cornerstone of our progress. His out-of-the-box ideas consistently provided fresh perspectives, enabling us to navigate complex challenges with creativity and confidence. Mark's ability to blend empathy with strategic thinking made him more than just a coach; he was a trusted ally on our journey. His insights and guidance were instrumental in helping us achieve our ambitious objectives. What sets Mark apart is his genuine dedication to our well-being, always ensuring that our professional growth is aligned with our personal values. The journey with Mark was not just about reaching a goal; it was about evolving as professionals and individuals, and for that, we are profoundly grateful."

The Mint Door

"Having been in sales my entire career, I began to think there was nothing new that would move the needle. The Goldman Enrollment Process is a game changer. Shifting the focus to the enrollment concept changes everything. If there was only one thing I could pass along to anyone looking for sales development, it would be this."

Buddy Hobart, Founder and CEO,
Solutions 21

"I have worked with David for many years. He has always focused on helping me develop *Mike's voice.* He has never tried to make me fit into a system. He takes best practices and helps me tailor them to my authentic style. He makes me the best possible, confident Mike. When you believe in yourself and your value, that's more than 90 percent of the game."

Mike Kauffelt,
Former CEO,
Bill Few Associates Wealth Management

"I have been in Mark's world for over twenty years. He is a remarkable coach and a wonderful friend. Without his support over these years, I do not know where I would be today. When I think of all the ways he has helped me one jumps to the front of the line. He helped me write my book *Now is Your Time: 31 Days to a More Extraordinary You*. This book is the story of my life and demonstrates God's love for me. Mark helped me to formulate the content and supported me through the publishing process. There is so much more, and he is simply the best!"

Elizabeth Hagen,
author of *Now Is Your Time*

"David has created a clear and meaningful process to help professionals grow their business, no matter the industry. I found his teachings to be applicable not only in my business's progress, but also my own personal development. As is the case with the best coaches in any industry (sports, sales, life, etc.), David worked with me to develop a system that highlighted my strengths, instead of forcing me into one set structure. What I learned has been tremendously useful and will continue to be for years to come."

John Nichols, CFP, Senior VP,
Bill Few Associates

"As a lawyer, I often had difficulty justifying my legal fees of several hundred dollars per hour, which equates to several dollars per minute. David taught me to value my expertise so that charging a significant amount of money was not only justified but correct. I went from being a bit timid about my legal fees to increasing them significantly by being very comfortable that

I am providing value far in excess of my fees. This transformation has not only made me more financially successful but also has made my legal career far more emotionally rewarding. Trust me, we can all learn a lot from David."

Ken Eisner, Principal,
Eisner Law Firm

With Henry's expertise and guidance, I set myself apart from the competition and built a multi-million-dollar consulting firm.

Tom Searcy,
founder of Hunt Big Sales and
co-author of *Whale Hunting and How To Close A Deal Like Warren Buffet*

"Without David's guidance, wisdom, listening skills, and most importantly his candor, I would not be in the position that I am in now in my career: that of enjoying what I do and earning more than I ever have. I equate David's coaching acumen to that of the great coaches in the sporting world over the years: he challenges you to be better by focusing on details that are right in front of us, but we choose to ignore. He challenges you to creatively market to your clients the *value proposition* for your services, and in the process abandon the old business models and methods of thinking. In short, without David's guidance over the past fifteen years, I would not have the quality of life that I have in balancing work and family. My only regret is not listening to David's advice sooner."

Michael W. Nalli, President, Nalli,
Elias & Associates PC

"Have you reached a plateau in your production and feel as though you are going nowhere fast? Face it: sometimes we are too far into the forest to see the trees. I've known David for nearly four decades. David Goldman can help you to overcome sales inertia. He lives for an opportunity to help others reach their goals. You have everything to gain."

Bernie Vukelich, CLU, CHfC, Principal,
Simplicity Group